RETIREMENT PLANNING

How to confidently make
the decisions needed to
accomplish your
retirement goals ...

by Maria Crawford Scott

Editor, *AAII Journal*

"The American Association of Individual Investors is an independent, not-for-profit corporation formed in 1978 for the purpose of assisting individuals in becoming effective managers of their own assets through programs of education, information, and research."

©Copyright 1998 by the American Association of Individual Investors. All rights reserved.

For more information about membership, contact:

American Association of Individual Investors
625 N. Michigan Avenue
Chicago, Ill. 60611
(312) 280-0170, (800) 428-2244
www.aaii.com
ISBN: 1-883328-11-X

CONTENTS

Introduction 1

Chapter 1: How Much of Your Salary Do You Need to Save for Retirement? 3
    Understanding Time and Money 3
    Guidelines for the Variables 4
    The Worksheet: Understanding the Approach 9
    Fixed Dollar Amounts 10
    The Salary Savings Tables 12
    Taking Aim 12

Chapter 2: What Will Be the Sources of Your Retirement Income? 15
    The Four Basic Sources 15
    Social Security 16
    Pension Plans 17
    Contributory Plans 19
    Personal Savings 20
    Taking Inventory of the Sources 21

Chapter 3: Investing Your Retirement Assets 25
    A Diversified Portfolio: Asset Allocation 25
    Portfolio Combinations 27
    Retirement vs. Taxable Investments 30
    Conclusion 32

Chapter 4: Some Reasons for Investing in 401(k) Plans 35
    Your Contributions Are Tax-Deferred 35
    Employer Matches and Other Advantages 37
    Should You Participate? 38
    The Bottom Line Decision 39

Chapter 5: How to Decipher Your 401(k) Plan Statements 41
    The Statement—An Example 41
    Vested Value: The Real Bottom Line 43
    Other Statement Information 44
    What Is Your Return? 44

Chapter 6: Understanding 401(k) Mechanics: A Look at How the Plans Operate 47
- Background 47
- Who Runs the Plan? 48
- What Documents Should Plan Participants Receive? 50
- What About Ongoing Information? 51
- What Problems Can Occur? 52
- What if You are Dissatisfied With the 401(k) Plan? 53
- Conclusion 53

Chapter 7: The ABCs of GICs in Retirement Investing 55
- GIC Basics 55
- GICs and 401(k) Plans 55
- Principal Risks—No Guarantee 56
- Newer Varieties 57
- Individual Investors and GICs 58
- Are GICs Appropriate? 59

Chapter 8: IRAs: One Other Retirement Choice 61
- Individual Retirement Accounts 61
- Spousal IRAs 62
- Non-deductible IRAs, Roth IRAs 62
- The Education IRA 63
- Choosing Your Options 64
- Summary 66

Chapter 9: Planning Considerations With the Roth IRA 69
- Annual Contributions 69
- Limitations On Converting 70
- Should You Convert? 71
- The Downside: Uncertainty 76
- Maximizing The Benefits 78
- Conclusion 78

INTRODUCTION

As Social Security teeters and 401(k) plans proliferate, more and more individuals recognize their own responsibility for ensuring their financial security in retirement.

How do you accomplish this? Proper planning is key: Saving enough each year, and investing your savings effectively so that they can grow and work for you to help you reach your long-term goals. This book provides the tools you need to plan for your retirement. It begins with a simplified worksheet in Chapter 1 that you can use to determine how much you need to save for your retirement. Chapter 2 discusses the sources of retirement income, pointing out the differences between employee retirement plans of younger and older workers. Chapter 3 delves into questions of how you should invest your retirement assets from an asset allocation point of view and which types of investments are well-suited for the tax-deferred status of retirement plans.

The next section of the book deals with 401(k) plans, a defined-contribution retirement plan offered by many employers today. Chapter 4 discusses the benefits of contributing to 401(k) plans as well as the possible drawbacks. Chapter 5 explains how to read and interpret your 401(k) plan statement and provides a simple formula to calculate the rate of return on your investments using the figures supplied in your plan statement. Chapter 6 describes the structure of 401(k) plans, showing how they work and what participants can expect from plan administrators. GICs (guaranteed investment contracts), a popular investment choice in many 401(k) plans, are covered in Chapter 7, with information on how these securities are set up and who may benefit from them.

The final two chapters deal with IRAs, detailing the different types and their features. The rules for deductibility are spelled out and comparisons of what each type of IRA would earn under sample tax rates help readers decide when a particular IRA may be appropriate for them.

As with all AAII products, this book provides unbiased education to help you become a better investor. Armed with the information in this book, you can confidently make the decisions needed regarding your retirement planning, a crucial aspect of investing for all individuals.

How Much of Your Salary Do You Need to Save for Retirement?

Two elements are essential to any savings plan: You must know how much you need, and you must know when you will need it.

When saving for specific purchases in the not-too-distant future—a new car or a house—those elements are relatively easy to determine. But for retirement planning, those elements aren't at all easy to figure out.

Financial planning worksheets can help individuals forecast those elements, but many are detailed and complicated; few individuals have the desire to work through these forms. The result: Most people throw up their hands and simply ignore the question entirely.

However, there is a simpler approach that you can use to come up with a reasonable retirement savings plan. There are limitations to the approach, and it is important that you understand those limitations and the assumptions used. For that reason, the amount of time it will take you to determine a reasonable savings plan will really be determined by how long it takes you to read and understand this chapter. After that, it will only take you a few minutes to work through the math in the worksheet, or to use the tables at the end of the chapter (for those with no current savings). The approach is designed to help you determine what percentage of your salary you need to set aside each year so that by retirement, you have accumulated enough savings to generate a desired real (inflation-adjusted) level of income during your retirement years.

Understanding Time and Money

There are two important concepts you must understand when dealing with time and money. The first is the power of compounding. When money is invested, it produces earnings that can then be reinvested, so that you receive earnings on your earnings in addition to the earnings on your original investment. This added boost is the power of compounding, and the longer the money is invested, the more powerful are its effects. Over long periods of time—20, 30, or 40 years—the effects of compounding at different rates can be substantial. For instance, if you invested $10,000 today and it earned 8% annually, you would have $100,626 at the end of 30 years; if it earned 9% you would have $132,676 after 30 years. That's a $32,000 difference with only a 1% difference in return annually.

You can see the advantages of earning higher returns over long time periods. But you must be very careful when making retirement plans that involve extremely long time periods—small differences in return assumptions can turn into large differences in accumulation. Be conservative in your estimates.

The second important concept concerns the value of a dollar today versus tomorrow. Over time, inflation erodes the worth of money, so that a given amount buys less in the future than it can today. When you are planning for the future, you are examining dollars over numerous time periods. To compare them, you need to put them on an equal purchasing-power footing, so they are all in equivalent dollar terms. In the approach used here, the equal footing will be the purchasing power of today's dollars—that is, dollar amounts will always be stated in terms of today's dollar equivalent.

Guidelines for the Variables

These are the variables you will need to determine when filling out the worksheet:
- The number of years you will spend in retirement,
- The number of years until you retire,
- Your total current savings,
- Your desired annual income in retirement, and
- The investment returns you expect on your savings.

Some of these are relatively straightforward, while others will require more thought. Here are some guidelines for determining the variables:

—Number of years in retirement

How long will you spend in retirement? The approach here assumes you will use up all of your savings in retirement, so the question boils down to how long you expect to live after you retire. The most common retirement age is 65; the average life expectancy at that age is around 17 years, but obviously many individuals live beyond that. If you plan to retire at age 65, assume a retirement period of at least 20 years, or longer to be more conservative.

—Number of years until retirement

How many years until you retire? This is pretty straightforward—it is the age at which you want to retire minus your current age.

—Total current savings

How much have you currently saved? This is also straightforward. It is simply the amount of savings you have accumulated up until now, either in taxable accounts or tax-deferred accounts such as individual retirement accounts or 401(k) plans.

—Desired annual income in retirement

What should you use as your desired annual income in retirement? While you could try to make an estimate of your needs, an easier method is to base the estimate on a percentage of your current gross, pretax salary (your resulting desired retirement income will also be pretax and your tax bracket is assumed to be the same both before and after retirement). Many retirement professionals suggest 80% as a benchmark; 100% of your current gross salary is a more conservative estimate. You do not need to adjust your desired income level for inflation; the tables will adjust it for you.

What about outside sources of income? At this point, you may want to subtract outside sources of retirement income such as Social Security and any pension benefits from defined-benefit plans (contributory plans, such as 401(k)s, should be considered savings); use the annual benefit stated in today's dollars. Estimates on your earned Social Security benefits can be obtained by filling out the Request for Earnings and Benefit Estimate Statement (to get a copy, call the Social Security Administration at 800/772-1213 and ask for the form). If you have any pension benefits, your employer's benefits department should provide you with an estimate. Be wary, however, of the Social Security situation, particularly if you will not be receiving benefits for many years, since significant changes may occur in benefit levels. You may want to leave it out.

—Expected return on savings

What rate of return should be used for savings, both before and after retirement? Your return will be a function of the mix of investments in your savings portfolio. For instance, if your savings are roughly divided evenly between stocks and bonds, your return would be 50% of the return from stocks plus 50% of the return from bonds.

Rates of return should be conservative and reasonable, preferably based on long-term historical averages. The box on the following page presents conservative estimates of returns for several major investment categories, based on historical returns over the past 50 years.

What about taxes? If most of your savings are in tax-deferred accounts, such as an individual retirement account or 401(k) plan, your return will be unaffected by taxes. However, if your savings are in taxable accounts, you should reduce your expected return to account for taxes. Taxes will have less of an impact on certain investments, such as stocks and low turnover stock mutual funds, since most of their return is due to long-term capital gains; taxes on these gains can be deferred until the asset is sold. Bonds and Treasury bills, however, are more affected by taxes, since most of their return is from income that is taxed annually. The table of return estimates provides rough guidelines for aftertax rates of return for individuals in the 15% and 28% tax brackets, assuming all returns for all categories are taxed annually, a very conservative assumption.

What if your savings are in both tax-deferred and taxable accounts? Do separate

Conservative Return Estimates
Based on the Past 50 Years

	Annual Return	Aftertax Return (28%)	Aftertax Return (15%)
Small Co. Stocks	12.0%	8.6%	10.2%
Large Co. Stocks	10.0%	7.2%	8.5%
Bonds	5.5%	4.0%	4.6%
Cash*	3.5%	2.5%	3.0%

*Treasury bills and money market funds

calculations for your taxable and tax-deferred savings, multiplying them by different savings growth factors based on the different return assumptions. Then add them together.

Will your returns be similar before and after retirement? Some individuals become more conservative after retirement, particularly as assets are drawn down and income and liquidity become more of a concern. On the other hand, it is important to keep some exposure to higher-return equities. You will have to decide what mix of investments you can live with at that stage.

Should you reduce your return expectations to take inflation into account? No. The tables already take inflation into account.

Retirement Savings Worksheet

Use this worksheet, along with Tables 1-4, to help determine how much you need to save for retirement. The guidelines in the text can help you determine the appropriate variables in the worksheet and tables.

Retirement Savings Needed:
Multiply your desired annual income in retirement by the Annuity Factor.

- Determine your desired annual income in retirement; if you want to take into consideration outside sources of retirement income (e.g., Social Security), subtract your expected annual benefits in today's dollars from your desired annual income.

- To find your Annuity Factor, look at the first column in Table 1 and find the number of years you expect to be in retirement; then go across until you find the rate of return you expect on your savings during retirement. The corresponding figure is your Annuity Factor.

- Line 1 tells you the value in today's dollars of the amount you will need to save by retirement in order to have the desired annual income in real terms for the number of years you are expected to be in retirement.

_____
(desired annual income)

× _____
(annuity factor from Table 1)

= _____
(line 1)

Current Savings:
Multiply your current savings by the Savings Growth Factor.

- To find your Savings Growth Factor, look at the first column in Table 2 and find the number of years until you will retire; then go across until you find the rate of return you expect on your savings during this period. The corresponding figure is your Savings Growth Factor.

- If you have both taxable and tax-deferred savings, do separate calculations for each (multiply each one by the relevant savings growth factor) and then add them together.

- Line 2 tells you the value in today's dollars of the amount your current savings will grow to by the time you retire.

_____
(current savings)

× _____
(savings growth factor from Table 2)

= _____
(line 2)

Retirement Savings Worksheet (continued)

Savings Shortfall:
Subtract Line 2 from Line 1.

- Line 3 tells you the value in today's dollars of the amount of your shortfall.

    _____ (line 1)
− _____ (line 2)
= _____
    (line 3)

Annual Savings:
Multiply Line 3 by the Annual Payment Factor.

- To find your Annual Payment Factor, look at the first column in Table 3 and find the number of years until you retire; then go across until you find the rate of return you expect on your savings during this period. The corresponding figure is your Annual Payment Factor.

- Line 4 is the value in today's dollars of the amount you need to save annually to make up the shortfall.

    _____ (line 3)

× _____
(annual payment factor from Table 3)

= _____
    (line 4)

Percentage of Salary You Need to Save Annually:
Divide Line 4 by your current salary

- The resulting figure is the percentage of your salary you need to save each year to make up the shortfall, assuming your salary keeps pace with inflation.

÷ _____
(current salary)

= _____ %
(percentage of salary)

Fixed Annual Savings
To convert savings into a fixed dollar amount:
Multiply Line 3 by the Fixed Dollar Payment Factor.

- To find your Fixed Dollar Payment Factor, look at the first column in Table 4 and find the number of years until you retire; then go across until you find the rate of return you expect to earn on your savings during this period. The corresponding figure is your Fixed Dollar Payment Factor.

- The resulting figure is the fixed dollar amount you need to save each year.

    _____ (line 3)

× _____
(fixed dollar payment factor from Table 4)

= $ _____
(fixed dollar amount)

The Worksheet: Understanding the Approach

The approach used in the worksheet is fairly straightforward, but it makes several assumptions. First, it assumes a 4% rate of inflation. It also assumes that all of your savings will be used up by the end of your retirement period. In the last step, it assumes that your annual salary will grow at the rate of inflation.

These are the basic steps in the approach:

- First, your desired annual income level in retirement is multiplied by an annuity factor (Table 1, on page 11), based on your number of years in retirement and the expected return on your savings in retirement. The resulting figure is today's dollar equivalent of the amount of savings you will need to accumulate by the time you retire to support your desired annual income level in real terms—in other words, your desired income level will grow with inflation to maintain its real value.
- Next, any current savings you may have is multiplied by the savings growth factor (Table 2), based on the number of years until retirement and the return you expect to earn on these savings. The resulting figure is today's dollar equivalent of the amount your current savings will grow to by the time you retire.
- Subtracting the amount you will have from the amount you will need indicates your shortfall—today's dollar equivalent of the amount you will need to save by the time you retire to support your desired annual income level.
- Next, the shortfall is multiplied by the annual payment factor (Table 3), based on the number of years until retirement and the return you expect to earn on your savings. The resulting figure indicates today's dollar equivalent of the amount you need to save annually to make up the shortfall by the time you retire.
- Lastly, dividing the annual savings amount by your current gross salary indicates the percentage of your salary that you need to save annually to make up for the shortfall by retirement to reach your retirement goal, assuming your salary increases with inflation.

As an example, let's assume that your current income is $35,000, your savings consists of $5,000 in an IRA, you are planning to retire in 35 years, and you expect to earn 8% on your savings both before and after retirement. You want to retire with an income level that will be equivalent to 80% of your current salary ($28,000) over your retirement period, which you are expecting to last 20 years:

- Your $28,000 desired income level multiplied by the Table 1 Annuity Factor of 14.31 equals $400,680.
- Your $5,000 current savings multiplied by the Table 2 Savings Growth Factor of 3.75 is $18,750.

- $400,680 minus $18,750 is $381,930, which is today's dollar equivalent of your shortfall, and the amount you still need to save.
- Your $381,930 shortfall multiplied by the Table 3 Annual Payment Factor of 0.013 is $4,965, today's dollar equivalent of the amount you need to save annually.
- $4,965 divided by your current salary of $35,000 is 14%—the percentage of your salary you need to save each year.

You may want to go through the worksheet several times using different variables—for instance, assuming different rates of return in your projections. This will illustrate the impact of these variables on your plans, and may prompt you to rethink some of your assumptions and perhaps even your plans. For instance, it will become clear that the earlier you start saving, the less you need to put aside each year; similarly, the more aggressively you invest for higher returns (within reason), the less you need to put aside annually.

Fixed Dollar Amounts

The approach in the worksheet provides you with an indication of the percentage of your salary that you need to save each year, the most commonly recommended way to save and the method used by many retirement plans, which are usually based on a percentage of one's salary.

However, some individuals may prefer to invest a fixed dollar amount each year, an amount that remains constant—for instance $5,000 each year, unadjusted for inflation. While the worksheet produces an annual savings amount, this is in today's dollars—an inflation-adjusted amount that maintains today's purchasing power; however, in future dollar terms, it increases each year by the inflation rate.

If you want to save a fixed dollar amount and still meet your stated retirement goal, the savings shortfall in the worksheet can be multiplied by a fixed dollar payment factor (Table 4), based on the number of years until retirement and the return you expect on your savings. The resulting figure is the fixed dollar amount you would need to save each year.

As an example, the savings shortfall in our example above was $381,930; multiplying this by the Table 4 fixed dollar annual payment factor of 0.023 produces $8,784, which is the amount that must be saved annually to reach the example's retirement goal.

Table 1. Annuity Factor

No. of Years in Retirem't	4%	6%	8%	10%	12%
20	20.00	16.79	14.31	12.36	10.82
25	25.00	20.08	16.49	13.82	11.80
30	30.00	23.07	18.30	14.93	12.48
35	35.00	25.79	19.79	15.76	12.95
40	40.00	28.26	21.03	16.39	13.28

Expected Return on Savings

Table 3. Annual Payment Factor

No. of Years to Retire	4%	6%	8%	10%	12%
5	0.200	0.189	0.178	0.168	0.159
10	0.100	0.090	0.081	0.073	0.065
15	0.067	0.057	0.049	0.041	0.035
20	0.050	0.041	0.033	0.026	0.021
25	0.040	0.031	0.024	0.018	0.013
30	0.033	0.024	0.018	0.012	0.009
35	0.029	0.020	0.013	0.009	0.006
40	0.025	0.017	0.011	0.006	0.004

Expected Return on Savings

Table 2. Savings Growth Factor

No. of Years to Retire	4%	6%	8%	10%	12%
5	1.00	1.10	1.21	1.32	1.45
10	1.00	1.21	1.46	1.75	2.10
15	1.00	1.33	1.76	2.32	3.04
20	1.00	1.46	2.13	3.07	4.40
25	1.00	1.61	2.57	4.06	6.38
30	1.00	1.77	3.10	5.38	9.24
35	1.00	1.95	3.75	7.12	13.38
40	1.00	2.14	4.52	9.43	19.38

Expected Return on Savings

Table 4. Fixed Dollar Annual Payment Factor

No. of Years to Retire	4%	6%	8%	10%	12%
5	0.225	0.216	0.207	0.199	0.192
10	0.123	0.112	0.102	0.093	0.084
15	0.090	0.077	0.066	0.057	0.048
20	0.074	0.060	0.048	0.038	0.030
25	0.064	0.049	0.036	0.027	0.020
30	0.058	0.041	0.029	0.020	0.013
35	0.054	0.035	0.023	0.015	0.009
40	0.051	0.031	0.019	0.011	0.006

Expected Return on Savings

If you have no current savings, Table 5 provides the bottom line answer regarding the percentage of your current salary that needs to be saved annually to reach certain retirement goals.

The Salary Savings Tables

If you have no current savings, Table 5 on page 13, provides the bottom line answer regarding the percentage of your current salary that needs to be saved annually to reach certain retirement goals. It includes:
- Percentages based on three different retirement scenarios: a retirement period lasting 20 years, one lasting 25 years, and one lasting 30 years.
- Percentages based on two different retirement income scenarios: one that is 100% of your current salary, and one that is 80% of your current salary.

For these scenarios, the tables indicate the percentage of your current salary that needs to be saved annually based on various assumed rates of return and the number of years until retirement. Use the guidelines presented above to determine which of these best fits your situation.

The assumptions underlying the tables are: a 4% average rate of inflation; salary and annual retirement income is pretax and both grow annually at the rate of inflation; the rate of return on savings is the same both before and after retirement; all savings are used up at the end of the retirement period.

As an example, let's assume an individual wants to retire on 100% of his current salary, expects to be retired for 25 years, has 30 years until retirement, and expects a return of 8% on his savings both during and after retirement. He would have to save 29% of his salary each year in order to generate an income level equal to 100% of his current salary for a 25-year retirement period.

In contrast, an individual with the same assumptions except that he expects annual returns of 10% would only have to save 17% of his salary each year. Even luckier is the individual who expects 10% returns but has 40 years until retirement—he would only have to save 9% of his salary each year.

The table illustrates a key point in retirement planning: It is much easier to achieve a desired retirement objective by starting early, and also investing aggressively. If you start late, meeting a particular retirement objective can consume an unrealistically large part of your annual income.

Taking Aim

Time plays a major factor in retirement guesstimates. The effects of compounding over a very long time period can mean big swings in results with only a small difference in assumptions.

Make sure you use conservative assumptions, but also understand that this planning device only provides a rough guide. It is impossible to predict with much accuracy how much you will need in retirement many years down the road, since all of the assumptions can change dramatically, including your own desires. Instead, aim for a general

Table 5. What Percentage of Your Salary Must You Save Annually?

Assumptions:
- 4% inflation
- Salary and retirement income is pretax
- Salary and annual retirement income grow with inflation
- All savings are used up
- Current savings are $0

Retirement Period: 20 years

If you want to retire at 100% of salary:

Years to Retire	4%	6%	8%	10%	12%
5	400%	317%	255%	208%	172%
10	200	151	116	90	70
15	133	96	70	51	38
20	100	68	47	33	23
25	80	52	34	22	14
30	67	41	25	15	9
35	57	33	19	11	6
40	50	28	15	8	4

If you want to retire at 80% of salary:

Years to Retire	4%	6%	8%	10%	12%
5	320%	254%	204%	167%	138%
10	160	121	92	72	56
15	107	77	56	41	30
20	80	55	38	26	18
25	64	42	27	18	11
30	53	33	20	12	8
35	46	27	15	9	5
40	40	22	12	6	3

Retirement Period: 25 years

If you want to retire at 100% of salary:

Years to Retire	4%	6%	8%	10%	12%
5	500%	379%	294%	233%	188%
10	250	181	133	100	77
15	167	115	80	57	41
20	125	82	54	36	25
25	100	62	39	25	16
30	83	49	29	17	10
35	71	40	22	12	7
40	63	33	17	9	5

If you want to retire at 80% of salary:

Years to Retire	4%	6%	8%	10%	12%
5	400%	303%	235%	186%	150%
10	200	144	107	80	61
15	133	92	64	46	33
20	100	65	43	29	20
25	80	50	31	20	13
30	67	39	23	14	8
35	57	32	18	10	5
40	50	27	14	7	4

Retirement Period: 30 years

If you want to retire at 100% of salary:

Years to Retire	4%	6%	8%	10%	12%
5	600%	436%	326%	251%	199%
10	300	207	148	108	81
15	200	132	89	62	44
20	150	94	60	39	26
25	120	71	43	27	17
30	100	56	32	19	11
35	86	46	25	13	7
40	75	38	19	10	5

If you want to retire at 80% of salary:

Years to Retire	4%	6%	8%	10%	12%
5	480%	348%	261%	201%	159%
10	240	166	118	87	65
15	160	105	71	49	35
20	120	75	48	31	21
25	96	57	35	21	13
30	80	45	26	15	9
35	69	37	20	11	6
40	60	30	15	8	4

savings target, and every few years review your assumptions and see if you can bring your target into closer focus.

Remember, when you do retire, you will have to adjust your lifestyle to your savings, rather than the other way around.

WHAT WILL BE THE SOURCES OF YOUR RETIREMENT INCOME?

Almost all investors would agree that providing for a comfortable retirement is a paramount financial objective. To plan properly, an investor needs to know:
- How much will be needed for retirement?
- What will be the sources for meeting that need?

Estimating your retirement needs, of course, is not an easy task. Chapter 1 provided a simplified approach to tackling this aspect. Equally difficult is the other half of the equation—sorting out where your retirement dollars will originate. Many investors have misperceptions of the various sources of their retirement income and the role each source will play at retirement. This is particularly true today because of the change occurring among employer-sponsored retirement plans and the possible declining role of Social Security. These misperceptions can be financially dangerous because they may cause investors to establish the wrong strategy for amassing sufficient funds for their golden years.

This chapter will explore the varied sources of an investor's retirement nest egg, what form it will come in (whether a monthly payment or lump sum) and how you can determine what to expect from each.

The Four Basic Sources

For most individuals, there are four basic retirement income sources: Social Security, employer-sponsored defined-benefit plans, tax-deferred savings plans such as 401(k)s, and personal savings.

How much you are likely to receive from each of these sources will vary greatly with personal circumstances, of course. In general, the percentage from each will depend on your age group. For instance, the bulk of the dollars for those 55 to 60 years old will come from Social Security and defined-benefit retirement plans, with a smaller amount from personal savings and 401(k)-type plans. Younger individuals will most likely fund their retirement from a dramatically different mix, with the 401(k) plans providing the majority of the dollars and Social Security and defined-benefit plans being a far smaller portion in the equation.

Let's look at the sources and what you can expect from each.

Social Security

The first retirement income source for most working individuals (and their spouses) is Social Security, which began during the late 1930s as a supplement to one's savings. It has since grown to represent, for many people, the bulk of their retirement income.

What can one expect to receive from Social Security at retirement? Benefits come in the form of monthly payments, based on your final years' salary and number of working years. You can get an estimate of your earned Social Security benefits by sending in Form SSA-7004 "Request for Social Security Earnings and Benefit Estimate Statement" to Social Security [800/772-1213 to request form]. The Statement lists your earnings for each year and provides an estimate of benefits, based on when you plan to retire (you are asked your retirement date when you fill out the request form). To calculate the estimate, Social Security must make a number of assumptions concerning future earnings; thus, the closer you are to retirement, the more realistic the estimate.

As a very rough idea, assume that a person is currently 45 years old and earns the maximum annual earnings subject to Social Security tax each year. At age 66 (the earliest age at which the person can retire and collect full monthly benefits) the retiree would receive $1,285 monthly (in today's dollars); while this is the maximum an individual could receive, benefits are also payable to dependents, which means a family could receive an additional 50%. For those who have maximum taxable earnings, Social Security is designed to replace roughly 25% of the portion of pay subject to Social Security taxes; individuals who have earnings that are less than the maximum subject to Social Security taxes receive a somewhat higher percentage of their final pay in the form of benefits.

There is considerable debate over the long-term financial stability of Social Security, and we will not go into the arguments here. However, younger individuals would be well-advised to de-emphasize Social Security for a number of reasons, all of which have the potential to reduce expected benefits.

First, there is continuing talk of raising the age at which a person may begin to receive full monthly benefits. This has already been done once: Those born in 1969 or later will find that they must wait until age 67 to collect their full monthly benefits.

There is also the possibility that the percentage of monthly benefits that are taxable to higher-income beneficiaries will be raised to 85%. Again, this has already occurred once—currently 50% of benefits are taxable to higher-income beneficiaries.

Lastly, there are some who propose denying benefits to anyone whose gross retirement income from all non-Social Security sources exceeds a certain amount. While this is still only a remote possibility, it could be the most damaging to one's financial health given the potential income one might have from other sources such as a well-funded 401(k) and personal savings.

It is for these reasons that a "baby boomer" should expect Social Security to play a minimal role in retirement planning. On the other hand, a person retiring in the next few years should manage to avoid most, but not all, of the negative effects of proposed changes in Social Security.

Pension Plans

Another potential retirement income source is employer-sponsored defined-benefit retirement plans—commonly called "pension" plans.

Benefits received under these plans are in the form of monthly payments, based on the employee's years of service and final years' salary. Monthly retirement benefits from defined-benefit plans may be paid either directly by the company, or from annuities purchased by the company.

Employees start accruing benefits (known as "vesting") after a certain number of years with a firm. Benefits under these plans are usually based on your years of service and either your average salary for the last five years or the last full year of employment; most plans then multiply the salary figure and the years of service by a percentage to calculate the actual amount at retirement. Pension plans are designed to replace only a portion of your salary upon retirement.

If your company sponsors a defined-benefit plan, you should check the rules regarding when you vest in the plan, the formula used to determine your monthly benefit (especially important for those who expect to retire soon), whether the plan has a cost-of-living adjustment for retirees (a few do), and the portability of your benefits. The latter offers employees considerable flexibility: Some defined-benefit plans have been modified recently to allow you to take the present value of some of your accrued benefits with you when you leave the company (a so-called "cash balance" plan). You then have the option of rolling this over into an IRA; if you have enough investment acumen, you may be able to grow these dollars to a higher level than would have accrued under the plan. Make sure you understand the tax rules regarding distributions and rollovers, however.

Some employers will give current employees an annual estimate of what they can expect to receive at retirement. The caveat is that the estimate makes certain assumptions: you will work at the same company until retirement and your salary increases by a certain fixed percentage (often only 3% or 4%).

If you leave a company before retirement and are vested in the firm's defined-benefit plan, you should request a calculation of the monthly benefits that could be expected at the normal retirement age. You should also make sure that you know who to contact in the human resources area at that company, and stay in touch with them every few years to ascertain any changes in the plan, and to inform them of any personal changes, such as a new address or marital status. This will keep your records up-to-date, and it will make it easier to file for benefits when first eligible. You should also know that a company is not legally obligated to keep in contact with a former employee who has a vested benefit and who leaves before retirement. It is thus incumbent on you to actively keep in contact.

Some former employees scoff at the idea of keeping in contact with their former employer, especially if they did not amass a potentially large dollar amount of defined-benefit assets. While the recordkeeping may seem onerous, everyone entitled to a monthly check from a defined-benefit plan should do whatever is necessary to be able to collect the owed money. The check may not be a windfall but every dollar counts.

While the idea of a steady stream of income is appealing, there are a number of less-than-obvious reasons why these plans may not deliver the benefits expected:

- Many workers fail to accrue meaningful benefits because they do not stay with one employer for long time periods. [While you may be "vested" in a plan (entitled to accrue and receive benefits), the level of benefits promised are based on the number of years employed by the firm and your final salary.]
- Most plans lack cost-of-living adjustments, which means inflation may erode the real value of the promised monthly payments.
- Companies may go out of business or have put aside insufficient assets to fund the plan. Participants in defined-benefit plans are offered some protection from this by the Employee Retirement Income Security Act (ERISA), passed in 1974, which set minimum funding standards and established the Pension Benefit Guarantee Corp. (PBGC). All companies with defined-benefit plans must pay a per employee premium to the PBGC, which assumes responsibility for pension plans when a company can no longer do so. However, benefits may be reduced somewhat under PBGC administration.
- The company may terminate its plan. When a plan is terminated, an employer will generally "annuitize" the vested benefits, purchasing annuities from an insurance company for those employees who are vested. The amount of the annuity is based upon the employee's current salary and service, and does not take into account his future years of service and salary increases. This will result in the employee receiving less money at retirement than he would have received had the plan not terminated. Some employers do not purchase annuities, but instead distribute the present value of the benefits accrued by vested employees, again based on the employee's current salary and service. The employee then has the option of rolling the money over into an IRA. Again, make sure you understand the tax implications of rollovers and distributions.

Defined-benefit plans are likely to play a larger role in older workers' overall retirement plan than in younger workers' plans. That's because many companies are terminating their plans due to the high expenses associated with them. In many instances, these plans are being replaced with contributory plans, such as 401(k)s. In addition, those in the younger age groups have a tendency to "hop" from one job to another every couple of years, which means that they will accrue minimal pension plan benefits at best, if at all.

Contributory Plans

Employer-sponsored contributory plans, such as 401(k) plans, have become increasingly common, and are most likely to play a large role in younger workers' retirement plans.

These employer-sponsored plans allow employees to invest pretax money in various investment alternatives chosen by the employer. Employers do not have to match an employee's contribution, although many do match part or all of what an employee puts into the plan.

Retirement benefits from a contributory plan come in the form of a lump-sum dollar amount upon retirement. The size of this amount will depend on the investment choices you make over the years, the amount contributed each year, and the number of years you participate. You can make a very rough calculation of your final amount by making an estimate of your annual contributions, the number of years to retirement and the approximate return you expect on your investments (based on your investment mix), and using an annuity table (the future value of a periodic investment).

Clearly, the size of your benefits depends on decisions you make within the limits of the choices offered. This has advantages as well as disadvantages. There is the potential in some employer's plans to make above-average long-term investment returns because of good investment options. On the other hand, poor investment returns will produce fewer dollars at retirement. In addition, the ultimate nest egg at retirement may not be big enough for a comfortable lifestyle if the employee did not start early enough and contribute as much as possible. And, of course, some plans may not offer a broad enough array of investment options.

If you are a participant in a 401(k)-type plan, you should make sure you understand the investment choices available, and you should carefully plan an investment strategy making best use of the options. You should also become familiar with the administrative rules governing the plan. While an employee has a vested right to the current value of the money he contributed, he may not have an immediate right to any contribution made by the employer. Often a plan states that the employer's contribution vests to the employee after a period of time—say, one year. Employees leaving one company for another should know exactly what they are entitled to from their plan. In addition, they should be aware of the tax rules regarding distributions and rollovers.

If you leave a company and have participated in a contributory plan, you may be allowed to keep your dollars in the plan. This can be beneficial if the plan has excellent investment options. Some plans, however, do not allow this. In either case, you have the option of rolling over these dollars into an IRA. In this case, you will generally have greater control over the money.

If you do leave a company and keep your assets in the plan, you should stay in contact with the human resources office to monitor changes in the plan and inform the company of any personal changes.

The recent development of 401(k)s means that older workers have not had an opportunity to save through the plans for a long time period, but younger workers have ample time to build a significant retirement nest egg.

Personal Savings

The last source for potential retirement income is personal savings. The need to fund other financial objectives before retirement often means that the amount put aside periodically for retirement is minimal; income taxes on taxable investments are also powerful obstacles to personal savings. In addition, reliance on personal savings could be for naught if an emergency or catastrophe causes the depletion of one's savings before retirement.

Yet for most people, the other sources of retirement income will not be enough on their own to meet retirement needs; they will have to be supplemented by personal savings. For the most part, your personal savings will consist of a lump-sum amount upon retirement, based on how much you have saved and where you have invested it. If you have purchased annuities, however, you will receive a monthly fixed payment.

There are two other often overlooked sources of retirement savings, although they should be used with caution. One is your home. If you do not intend to stay in your home after retirement and intend to live in less expensive quarters, you could sell your house and use the difference between the sales proceeds and the cost of your new home; up to $250,000 of gain ($500,000 married filing joint) can be excluded from taxes. Another possibility is a reverse mortgage, which will give you periodic income from the house. Be sure that you fully understand the implications of either selling your house or taking a reverse mortgage before you proceed with the transaction.

Another possible source is the cash value of a life insurance policy, since your need for life insurance usually is small upon retirement. However, if you are using life insurance as an estate planning device, you should make sure that any contemplated surrender does not negate the work you have done to avoid or reduce inheritance taxes.

Taking Inventory of the Sources

If you are attempting to build a retirement plan, you must take financial inventory of your retirement income sources. This entails knowing what dollar amounts you will receive at retirement. You must also know certain information about each source of retirement income, such as how it will be taxed in your retirement years, and other characteristics.

One way of analyzing your retirement sources is by dividing them into sources of periodic income and sources of lump-sum assets upon retirement. The latter would supplement the former to the extent that further retirement income is needed.

Table 1 details the sources of periodic income, showing their tax characteristics at retirement and other features. Social Security and defined-benefit plans will begin paying at retirement age once the retiree has given proper notice. Individual annuities bought from personal savings will begin distributing the money based upon the initial distribution date specified in the annuity contract. Note that IRAs are listed as a

Table 1. Sources of Periodic Income

	Tax Characteristics at Retirement	Cost-of-Living Adjustments	Long-Term Viability
Social Security	Part of benefit may be taxable	Annual, but may be changed by Congress	Don't count on it
Defined-Benefit Plan	Taxable as income when received	Some plans	Many workers do not stay long enough to accumulate meaningful benefits
Individual Annuity	Part of distribution is taxable	None	For fixed annuities, implied return may not keep up with inflation. For variable annuities, need to closely monitor the investment choices and your strategy.
Deductible IRA (after age 70 ½)	Taxed as income when received; penalties for not withdrawing enough	Depends on investor's strategy	Good source for long-term savings; build up if possible

Table 2.
Sources of Lump-Sum Assets

	Tax Characteristics at Retirement	When to Use to Supplement Retirement Income
Taxable Savings	Realized gains and investment income are taxed each year.	Use this first, especially if your marginal tax rate is higher than the capital gains tax rate.
Deductible IRAs	Taxes on gains and income deferred until distributions made; payouts taxed as income.	Defer using this source as long as possible to take advantage of tax-deferred status. Must begin to take distributions by age 70½.
Lump-Sum Retirement Distributions	Special averaging is currently available; or roll over into IRA.	Use first (similar to taxable savings) if averaging is used; otherwise treat it as IRA.
Sale of House	Exclusion of $250,000 ($500,000 married filing joint) from capital gains taxes.	Use in place of other non-taxable sources if needed.
Sale (Surrender) of Life Insurance Policy	Taxable as income if cash received exceeds premiums paid less dividends.	Use in place of other non-taxable sources; make sure you do not need the insurance for estate planning purchases.

periodic income source after age 70½, since you are required to start distributions from them at this time.

Table 2 highlights sources of lump-sum assets at retirement. This would consist of personal savings you have accumulated through the years, as well as lump-sum distributions from employer-sponsored contributory plans. The table also indicates tax characteristics at retirement, and the likely order of use as income sources to maximize tax characteristics. In most cases, taxable savings should be used first for retirement income, as long as your marginal tax rate exceeds the capital gains rate. However, decisions on initiating withdrawals from deductible IRAs and lump-sum retirement distributions must be made carefully to avoid distribution and taxation until the retiree is forced financially to begin the process.

What steps should you take to beef up your sources?

For older workers (for instance, those in the 55 to 60 age group):
- You cannot do very much about your Social Security or defined-benefit sources—which at least will probably be there for your retirement. The only aspect of Social Security you will need to examine is whether you can wait to collect your benefits at the normal retirement age or whether you need the reduced benefits that are currently available at age 62. Many people retire from their jobs in their early 60s and find that they must elect early Social Security benefits in order to supplement their income. Not doing the necessary arithmetic well beforehand can result in an incorrect decision.
- If you expect to work for several more years, maximize your use of a 401(k) and choose investment options that offer some growth of capital with moderate risk. The current level of interest rates means that GICs (guaranteed investment contracts—see Chapter 7) might provide a return around 6.0%; a balanced fund option might give you higher returns with more risk. An aggressive stock fund should be avoided because of the high volatility associated with that investment and the limited time available to recover from a market decline.
- Personal savings should be maximized, but a caveat is required regarding tax-free securities: If you plan to hold them while you are collecting Social Security remember that you must include all of your tax-free income when calculating the possible tax on Social Security benefits.

For younger workers:
- Realize that you must place a far lower reliance on Social Security and defined-benefit dollars for retirement.
- The significance of 401(k) plans means that you must make the most of these plans, contributing the maximum amount that you can and investing for the long term. This means equity investment, especially growth stock vehicles if they are available.
- Personal savings must be maximized to make up for the diminished dollars from Social Security.

The changing mix of retirement income sources necessitates that each investor explore his personal financial circumstances and plan accordingly. What was true for former and current retirees will not be true for future retirees.

Investing Your Retirement Assets

Achieving a comfortable lifestyle in those golden retirement years can be a daunting objective these days. Retirements will last far longer than in the past. However, the task is not insurmountable. Knowing how to invest your savings will go a long way in helping you meet your retirement goals.

Most individuals, though, will also be saving for other goals during their lifetimes—for instance, a house, or tuition for their child's education. The most efficient investment portfolios are based on an overall approach that examines the risk and return potential of your total portfolio, not just the individual parts. That means looking at all of your investable assets as a whole, including those that may be in a retirement account such as an IRA or an employer-sponsored 401(k) plan, as well as other savings.

Your total investment portfolio should match your investment profile, which includes your risk tolerance, your return needs, time horizon, and tax exposure. To structure the portfolio, the process starts at the top and works its way down, first allocating among the major asset categories, then within each of those asset categories.

A Diversified Portfolio: Asset Allocation

The first portfolio task faced by any individual is to set up an overall framework for the investment of your portfolio. This framework is built around your own personal investment profile, taking into consideration your return needs and your tolerance for risk. Another term for this is *asset allocation,* which consists of dividing your portfolio up among the major asset categories of stocks, bonds and cash.

Although asset allocation may seem simple—after all, you are only choosing among three categories—the decisions you make here will have a far greater impact on your overall portfolio return than any other more specific decision that you may make about your portfolio (assuming, however, that you follow basic investment principles in your other decisions, the most important of which is that you remain diversified among and within the various investment segments).

How does one set up an investment framework?

The first step is to understand how the various aspects of your personal profile can affect your investment decisions. The most important considerations are: your tolerance for risk, your return needs, and your time horizon. Here's how your personal

Table 1.
The Personal Investment Profile

Factors	Range
Risk Tolerance: How much of a loss can you stomach over a one-year period without abandoning your investment plan?	• Low: 0% to 5% loss • Moderate: 6% to 15% loss • High: 16% to 25% loss
Return Needs: What form of portfolio return do you need to emphasize: a steady source of income, growth, or a combination?	• Income: Steady source of annual income • Growth/Income: Some steady annual income, but some growth is also needed • Growth: Growth to assure real (after inflation) increase in portfolio value
Time Horizon: How soon do you need to take the money out of your investment portfolio?	• Short: 1 to 5 years • Long: Over 5 years

investment profile is likely to look:

Risk tolerance. The amount of risk you are willing to take on is important because if you take on too much risk, you could panic and abandon your plan; usually this occurs at the worst possible time.

The best measure of risk is to ask yourself how much of a loss you can stomach over a one-year period without bailing out of your investment plan. In general, investors with a low tolerance for risk can sustain losses of no more than 5% over a one-year time period; investors with a moderate risk tolerance can withstand total losses of between 6% to 15%; and investors with a high risk tolerance can withstand losses of between 16% to 25% annually.

Individuals in their working years and saving for retirement can be more tolerant of risk because they are not relying on their portfolio for income, and because they have time to rebuild a portfolio should a significant loss occur. Investors closer to retirement tend to become less tolerant of risk.

Whatever your own tolerance for risk may be, it is important not to have zero tolerance—some downside risk must be tolerated in order to incorporate a growth element into the portfolio to sustain its real value against the eroding effects of inflation. Higher growth, and therefore higher return, can only be achieved by taking on higher risk.

Return needs. This refers to the type of portfolio return you need to emphasize: A steady source of annual income, a high but variable growth potential, or a combination of the two. Determining your return needs is important because of the trade-off between income and growth: The price for a steady annual payment is lower growth potential.

Younger investors tend to need only growth, while those nearing retirement may have a combination of growth and income needs. In any portfolio, some growth is needed to ensure that the value of your portfolio keeps pace with inflation; the minimum growth needed to do this would be the expected inflation rate.

Growth investments also needn't be ruled out when considering income needs. Dividend income is usually lower than bond income at any given point in time, and dividends are also less assured than bond yields, but the long-term average is not unattractive, and that yield is a percentage on an increasing amount, since the underlying value of the stock will grow.

Time horizon. Your time horizon starts whenever your investment portfolio is implemented and ends when you will need to take money out of your investment portfolio. The time horizon is important because stocks are very volatile over short periods of time and are therefore inappropriate as short-term investments. In general, a short-term time horizon is less than five years and a longer-term time horizon is over five years.

For most younger investors saving for retirement, the time horizon is long-term.

However, even young investors may have a short-term time horizon for a portion of savings—if, for instance, saving for the down payment on a house. The short-term horizon encompasses liquidity needs. Cash provides a liquidity pool, and to the extent that resources are for more immediate needs, this section of the portfolio should be increased to avoid any necessity to sell long-term investments unexpectedly.

Portfolio Combinations

The next step is to examine various possible portfolio combinations to see how they might fit your personal investment profile. To do this, you should examine the risk and return potential characteristics of these combinations.

Table 2 presents risk and return characteristics for the three major asset categories. The figures are based on long-term annual averages for total return, annual capital growth and current yield, but it is important to keep in mind that these are long-term averages and significant year-to-year variations can be expected to occur. For downside risk, the figures are based on the worst loss over a one-year holding period during severe bear market conditions.

To help judge your tolerance for risk, use the downside risk figures as a guide to how much of a loss you can stomach. The average annual returns, broken down between growth and income, can be used to help assess your growth and income needs. Downside risk also serves as a guide to your time horizon, illustrating the risk involved with short-term time periods.

What do the figures show?

- Stocks contain the only real growth element, but this is achieved at high risk, with the possibility of a significant loss (–25%) during bear markets. Of course, this assumes that you are investing in a well-diversified portfolio of stocks that includes growth stocks and the stocks of smaller firms.
- Bond investments, and to a lesser extent cash (money market funds), offer steadier sources of income, but no potential for growth.
- Cash investments, with no downside risk, offer liquidity and the ability to temper the overall downside risk of a portfolio. This component should be used for short-term investment horizons. On the other hand, the risk/return equation increasingly favors stocks over longer holding periods. In Table 2, the worst-case scenario for a one-year period is illustrated but, historically, the longer the holding period, the less likely you are to sustain a substantial loss in a stock portfolio. In other words, the worst-case scenario for stocks decreases for longer holding periods, and particularly for holding periods longer than five years.

Table 2.
Risk and Return Characteristics for Three Major Asset Categories

	Total Annual Return*	Average Annual Growth*	Average Annual Income*	Downside Risk**
Stocks	11%	8%	3%	–25%
Bonds	7%	0%	7%	–5%
Cash	4%	0%	4%	0%

*Based on long-term average estimates for total return, annual capital growth, and current yield; however, significant year-to-year variation can be expected.

**An annual decline based on severe bear market conditions.

Table 3.
Risk and Return Characteristics for Combination Portfolios

Portfolios (stocks/bonds/cash)	Total Annual Return (%)	Average Annual Growth (%)	Average Annual Income (%)	Downside Risk* (%)
Conservative (50%/40%/10%)	8.7	4.0	4.7	−14.5
Moderate (60%/30%/10%)	9.1	4.8	4.3	−16.5
Aggressive (80%/0%/20%)	9.6	6.4	3.2	−20.0

*An annual decline based on severe bear market conditions. For the portfolios it assumes the worst-case assumption that diversification fails and all categories decline at the same time.

The three major asset categories can be combined to produce any number of portfolios that can meet the needs of any investor profile. Table 3 presents the risk and return potential characteristics of three possible combinations.

How are these numbers derived?

The averages for each category in Table 2 are multiplied by the percentage allocated to each category and then added together. For instance, the conservative portfolio consists of 50% in stocks, 40% in bonds, and 10% cash. The average annual return is:

$$(50\% \times 11) + (40\% \times 7) + (10\% \times 4) = 8.7\%$$

The downside risk for the combination portfolios assumes the worst-case scenario—that all three categories are down at the same time, a very conservative assumption that diversification has failed.

The conservative portfolio emphasizes bonds for a steady annual income of 4.7%, while the 50% commitment to stocks provides a growth element of 4%, and also allows the income component to keep pace with inflation. The downside risk of −14.5% is the lowest of the three portfolios, close to the moderate range.

The second combination provides a more moderate mix that increases the stock component to 60%, decreases the bond component to 30%, and is 10% in cash. This provides a lower level of income than the conservative portfolio, but it provides at least a minimum of real growth in portfolio value, which also allows the income component to grow in real terms. The price is an increase in downside risk from the first combination.

The aggressive portfolio consists of 80% in stocks and 20% in cash. It does not supply a steady income, but the growth potential is quite large and more than makes up for the loss in steady income—at 6.4%, this provides a real (above inflation) growth of 2.4%, assuming inflation of 4%, and allows the income component to grow as well. However, the price is an even steeper rise in downside risk—a loss of about 20% in the worst-case scenario. The 20% commitment to cash may seem high, but it tempers the downside risk. Alternatively, 10% could be shifted from cash to bonds to increase income, with a slight increase in downside risk.

The sample portfolios here are simply examples—there are any number of combinations that are available to meet the various investment profiles. You need to decide for yourself which combination best suits your needs and risk tolerance.

Retirement vs. Taxable Investments

In our current tax structure, "retirement" account is a misnomer. That is, you should not think of your assets as consisting of "retirement" savings and "regular" savings; instead think of your assets as consisting of a tax-deferred portion and a taxable portion.

The question of where you should invest "retirement money," whether it be in a 401(k) plan, 403(b) plan, IRA, or some other retirement account, is really a tax-planning decision that is determined after you have decided on the composition of your total investment portfolio. Once you have decided on your portfolio composition, you can then allocate the chosen investments in such a way as to minimize taxes. Of course, if you are in an employer-sponsored plan, your investment choices will also be limited by the selections provided by your employer. But assuming the selections are satisfactory and cover all investment categories, the decision comes down to taxes.

At first glance, the decision as to which kinds of investments to allocate to taxable and tax-deferred accounts would appear to be simple: Shelter the investments generating the higher amount of annual taxable income, and put those investments that generate gains into taxable accounts.

When it comes to taxes, however, nothing is ever simple.

Any investment with high annual returns—whether from income, dividends or realized capital gains—benefits from deferring taxes, and the longer the deferral, the more those benefits are able to compound.

Taxes in tax-deferred accounts are deferred until the assets are withdrawn, at which time they are taxed as income at ordinary income tax rates. In the case of investments with capital gains, the advantage of the lower capital gains tax rate is lost if the asset is placed in a tax-deferred account. However, the advantages of deferring taxes are strong, and when allowed to compound over long time periods—15 to 20 years—they can overwhelm higher tax rates that must be paid on withdrawal for many investors.

The best of both worlds, of course, is an investment in which you can defer paying taxes, but which is then taxed at the capital gains rate. This can be accomplished if you hold individual stocks, since you have complete control of the timing decision as to when to sell and realize gains. Many individuals, though, do not hold onto individual stocks for time periods as long as 15 to 20 years.

Most stock mutual funds—even those that have very low portfolio turnover—produce at least some annual distributions. Studies indicate that even low distribution levels on an annual basis tend to tip the scales in favor of tax-deferred accounts for high-returning stock mutual funds.

As a rule of thumb, a tax-efficient portfolio is allocated as follows:
- The tax-deferred portion consists of higher-returning investments. Thus, if you hold both stock and bond mutual funds, the stock funds should be allocated to the tax-deferred portion since they tend to produce much higher average annual rates of return, even though bond funds tend to have larger annual distributions. If you hold several kinds of stock funds, those that tend to have higher average annual rates of return should be allocated to the tax-deferred portion—for instance, if you hold both aggressive growth and equity-income funds, the aggressive growth funds should be allocated to the tax-deferred portion, since they tend to produce higher annual returns.
- The taxable portion consists of lower-returning investments, such as balanced funds and bond funds; investments in which you have complete control over the timing decision and that you are likely to hold onto for long time periods, such as long-term individual stock holdings; and investments with built-in tax shelter advantages, such as municipal bonds.

In addition, there are a number of investments that should not be held in a retirement account. These include:

- *Use of Leverage*
  Be aware that in an IRA, any interest, dividends, rents, etc., will be taxable to the extent that it is generated by assets acquired or improved through the use of debt. This includes the purchase of publicly traded shares of stocks or bonds on margin.
- *Collectibles*
  If you invest in collectibles using IRA dollars, the purchase will be deemed a fully taxable distribution subject to the 10% penalty tax (assessed on IRA distributions made prior to your age 59½, with some limited exceptions).

"Collectibles" include the following: art, gems, musical instruments, rugs, stamps, historical objects, antiques, coins, wines or other collectible alcoholic beverages, metal, or any other item of tangible personal property the IRS determines to be a collectible.

The only exception to the above is gold or silver coins minted by the U.S., acquired after December 31, 1986; or coins issued under the laws of any state if acquired after November 10, 1988.

- *Municipal Bonds*

  The primary benefit of municipal bonds—including those in tax-exempt bond mutual funds—is that their interest payments are exempt from federal (and possibly state) income taxes. Because of this benefit, the interest rates earned are less than what could be earned on a taxable bond with similar characteristics, such as term and quality. Putting a municipal bond into an IRA eliminates the tax-exempt nature of the interest, so you receive a lower rate of interest with no tax advantage. Although tax-deferred, the earnings will be fully taxable upon distribution from the IRA.

- *Annuities*

  Insurance company annuities allow for the deferral of tax on earnings from these investments by virtue of special income tax provisions. In return for this benefit, the investor makes a long-term commitment to the insurance company and may pay fees in excess of alternative investment options. Obviously, if the primary benefit of the annuity is its tax-deferred status, it loses some appeal as an IRA investment. When non-IRA assets are available for investment, it would be best to purchase the annuity outside, rather than inside, the IRA. If non-IRA assets are not available, review carefully the purported benefits of such an investment inside your IRA.

Conclusion

Here are some points to keep in mind when developing an investment plan for your retirement savings:

- First, develop an investment plan for all of your investable assets, based on your own needs and tolerance for risk.
- A commitment of at least 50% in stocks will most likely be needed in any portfolio to provide growth and prevent loss in real terms of the value of your portfolio. However, the stock portfolio must be adequately diversified and include some commitment to the stocks of smaller firms, as well as international stocks.
- Downside risk is a good way to judge risk tolerance, but keep in mind that some downside risk must be tolerated to allow a growth component in your

portfolio.
- Bonds provide income but no growth component. They also produce some downside risk. This downside risk can be reduced by keeping maturities on the shorter end (five to seven years) of the spectrum.
- Cash should be used to provide enough liquidity so that you are not forced to sell investments at inopportune times.
- Cash can also be used to moderate the downside risk introduced by a large stock component.
- Try to shelter investments with the highest returns in tax-deferred retirement accounts, such as IRAs and 401(k) plans.
- Investments with lower returns should be relegated to the taxable portion of your portfolio.
- Investments with built-in shelters, such as municipal bonds, and short-term liquid investments that are set aside for emergencies should never be placed in a tax-deferred retirement account.

Some Reasons for Investing in 401(k) Plans

The fastest-growing type of retirement plan offered by corporations today is the 401(k), named after the section of the Internal Revenue Code that created them. A similar plan, the 403(b), is often offered to employees of non-profit organizations.

These plans are a type of retirement plan referred to as defined contribution—the ultimate benefits that are paid out depend on the level of contributions made to the plan and the investment performance of those contributions. And in most plans, these two important decisions—how much to contribute and where to invest the contributions—are made by the employee.

Some surveys indicate that many employees don't fully understand the advantages these plans can offer. On the other hand, there are occasions when certain disadvantages outweigh the advantages to some employees.

Let's look at the advantages of these retirement plans and when you should—and in some instances, should not—participate.

Your Contributions Are Tax-Deferred

One of the most important advantages of a 401(k) plan is tax-deferral on both contributions and earnings.

Contributions to a 401(k) plan by the employee are made on a pretax basis (although some plans allow for additional contributions on an aftertax basis). Pretax contributions are those that are taken from your salary before income taxes for the year are determined. The result is a lower tax bill in the year that contributions are made.

This doesn't mean that the contributions are tax-free. Instead, you pay taxes when the money is withdrawn from the plan, usually at retirement. In other words, taxes on your contributions and on the earnings (interest, dividends, and capital gains) are deferred. However, the money builds up more quickly than would be the case if you invested aftertax money and paid taxes each year on the earnings.

For example, let's assume that you earn a salary of $45,000 a year, and that you plan to contribute $3,000 to your 401(k) plan this year. The W-2 form you would receive for that tax year would list an income of $42,000, rather than $45,000; as a result, your tax bill, assuming a 28% tax bracket would be lower by $840 ($3,000 × 28%) than if you had not made the contribution.

If you invest that same amount of money each year, earning 8% annually, for 20

Table 1.
401(k) Plan Accumulations vs. Taxable Savings
($3,000 pretax salary invested annually;
8% pretax rate of return; 28% tax bracket)

No. of Yrs.	401(k) Plan Accumulations* Before Taxes ($)	401(k) Plan Accumulations* After Taxes ($)	Taxable Savings** ($)	Difference In Savings ($)
5	19,008	13,686	12,816	870
10	46,936	33,794	29,773	4,021
15	87,973	63,340	52,210	11,130
20	148,269	106,754	81,897	24,857
25	236,863	170,542	121,178	49,364
30	367,038	264,267	173,152	91,115
35	558,306	401,981	241,921	160,060
40	839,343	604,327	332,912	271,415

*Accumulations are not subject to any early withdrawal penalties.
** Assumes annual taxation of all earnings, a 5.76% aftertax return; if savings were invested in instruments that allowed some deferral, such as those generating long-term capital gains, taxable savings would be higher.

years, it would grow to $148,269. If you then withdrew the money from the plan, you would owe $41,515 in taxes ($148,269 × 28%) for an ending value of $106,754.

What if you don't contribute to a 401(k) plan but instead save aftertax money each year? First, you would only have $2,160 to invest, since you would have had to pay taxes on the $3,000. In addition, your 8% annual return could turn into a 5.76% aftertax return, since you may have to pay taxes on the earnings, such as interest and dividend income, each year. (If your investment is in a vehicle that produces capital gains, where taxes can be deferred and rates are lower, your aftertax rate would be somewhat higher.) After 20 years, your investment would grow to $81,897 (assuming the 5.76% aftertax rate).

The $24,857 difference represents the real advantage of deferring taxes on both income and earnings. The table above illustrates the differences over various time periods, assuming a $3,000 pretax annual investment, an 8% pretax rate of return and a 28% tax bracket.

The tax-deferral aspect also gives you flexibility to determine the best time to pay the tax, with the possibility that when you eventually do pay taxes, it will be at a lower rate.

Employer Matches and Other Advantages

The other major advantage of many 401(k) plans is employer-matched contributions. For instance, an employer may contribute $0.50 for every $1 that you contribute to the plan. This is an obvious advantage—you are earning 50% on your contribution before you have even invested it anywhere.

This advantage depends in part on any cap the employer may have on the match. And the advantage depends on the employer's vesting requirements. Vesting is the right an employee gradually acquires to receive employer-contributed benefits, and is based on the length of time employed. The faster the vesting period, the more advantageous the employer-matched contribution, unless you plan to stay with the company (or have been with the company) for the full vesting time period.

There are several other important advantages offered by 401(k) plans. They include:

- *Flexibility:* You can determine the amount you are able to contribute, and you make the decisions as to where your money is invested. Most plans permit periodic transfers among the available investment choices.
- *Portability:* If you should leave your employer, any contributions you have made to your plan, as well as their earnings, are yours; *vested* contributions made to your plan by your employer are also yours. At this point, if you transfer these contributions to a new employer's plan or into an IRA, no penalties are incurred and no taxes are due until you take a distribution (make sure you understand the rollover rules, however, particularly those regarding withholding, since mistakes will incur costly penalties). On the other hand, if you take a distribution (by not transferring to a new employer's plan or an IRA), taxes will be due and you will have to pay a 10% early distribution penalty if you are below age 59½.
- *Periodic investing made easy:* An automatic deduction from your paycheck allows you to invest right from the start without any action on your part. And periodic payments allow you to gradually build up your investment without having to make big financial sacrifices. The benefits of starting an investment program early are considerable, due to the power of compounding. When you invest, your money produces interest or capital gains; those earnings can then be reinvested so that you receive earnings on your earnings. The longer you allow the compounding effect to work, the more your money earns on its own.

Table 2.
Return Needed from Taxable Savings to Match Aftertax Accumulation in 401(k) Plan*

Tax Rate	Expected Return from 401(k) Plan		
	6.0%	8.0%	10.0%
15.0%	7.1%	9.4%	11.8%
28.0%	8.3%	11.1%	13.9%
31.0%	8.7%	11.6%	14.5%
36.0%	9.4%	12.5%	15.6%

*Assumes 401(k) plan accumulations are not subject to 10% penalty for early withdrawal. Also assumes returns from taxable savings are taxed annually.

Should You Participate?

The advantages described previously are strong arguments in favor of participating in your company's 401(k) plan. Tax-deferral alone is a compelling reason that will enable you to build your retirement nest egg much more quickly than if you were to do so on your own. An employer-match program, if your employer offers one, is also a powerful incentive to participate. For most individuals, the positives outweigh the negatives. But you still should be aware of some of the disadvantages of 401(k) plans.

First, you have limited access to your money for a long period of time, and the immediate access that you do have could come at a high price—the 10% penalty for early withdrawal. This penalty, of course, works against the advantages of tax-deferral.

For the most part, your 401(k) plan money will remain in the plan until you retire or leave the company. Once you reach age 59½, you can receive distributions from your 401(k) plan without penalty, although you must pay taxes on the distribution.

If you leave the company and you have not reached 59½, you can take a lump-sum distribution of your 401(k) plan money to spend as you wish but only by paying a 10% early withdrawal penalty and, of course, taxes; you can avoid the penalty only by rolling your money over into an IRA or a new employer's qualified plan.

Access to your 401(k) money when you remain with your employer isn't entirely restricted, just limited. Some plans allow participants to borrow funds from their 401(k) plan assets, usually at an intermediate-term market rate. Borrowers are in effect loaning money to themselves and repaying the loan into their 401(k). However, loans that are not repaid within the restricted time period are considered distributions, with taxes and a 10% early withdrawal penalty due.

In addition, some companies will permit withdrawals from a 401(k) plan due to severe financial hardships. However, anyone requesting part or all of their dollars under this clause must show their employers that they have exhausted all other non-retirement financial resources. These withdrawals are also subject to the 10% early withdrawal penalty, and taxes must be paid on the distribution.

These features are comforting for short-term emergencies. However, to take full advantage of your employer's 401(k) plan, you should consider money invested in the plan to be long-term savings.

A second possible drawback is that you are limited to the investment choices provided by the employer. This may or may not be a negative. Most employers provide at least one form of investment in three broad asset categories—cash, bonds, and stocks. And many employers provide a number of choices within those categories.

But what if you are uncomfortable with or strongly dislike your employer's selection(s)? For instance, if you have only limited funds for savings, and you dislike your employer's stock fund selection, would you be better off investing your limited funds in a taxable account, or are you better off contributing to an employer plan even if you feel it will provide lower returns?

Clearly, in this instance there is a trade-off between the tax-deferral advantages of the 401(k) plan and the higher returns you may feel you can find elsewhere. A rough guide to this trade-off is provided on the opposite page in Table 2, which shows the return you would need to earn in a taxable savings account (assuming all earnings are taxed as income each year) to accumulate the same amount as the aftertax value of a 401(k) plan that has lower expected returns.

If your taxable savings were invested in instruments that produce primarily long-term capital gains where taxes can be deferred, the necessary rate of return would be somewhat less than illustrated. The table assumes that the 401(k) plan accumulations are not subject to the 10% early withdrawal penalty. The table also does *not* take into consideration any employer-matching program, which tilts the odds more heavily in favor of the 401(k) plan.

The Bottom Line Decision

Should you participate in your employer's 401(k) plan? The advantages are very strong and include:
- Your contribution is pretax and reduces your taxes in the year that the contribution is made. You will, of course, eventually have to pay taxes.
- The tax-deferral aspect allows you to build up your retirement nest egg more quickly than otherwise.
- It is an easy form of periodic investing that allows a gradual but steady buildup of your savings over time.
- If your company matches your contributions, you are getting a free boost from

your employer.

What would be reasons not to contribute to the plan?
- Liquidity: You are sure that you will need the money to spend sometime in the near future (for instance, in five years or less), or
- You are uncomfortable with all of the investment options and feel that you can earn a better return in a taxable savings account, even after taking taxes into consideration (and assuming there is no employer match).

How to Decipher Your 401(k) Plan Statements

While 401(k) plans are popular, they are also a source of confusion. Employers furnish participants with periodic statements detailing the value of the employee's plan and other account information. But many participants are uncertain how to interpret the statements.

Unfortunately, there is no standardized plan statement—most, in fact, are quite different. However, Figure 1 (based on a statement supplied by the Vanguard Group) should give you an idea of some of the information that may be included, even if it appears in a different format.

The Statement—An Example

The statement in Figure 1 is divided into several sections: activity this period, current contributions allocation, and a summary of contributions.

For most participants, the first section describing activity during the most recent period is the most relevant.

In the example in Figure 1 account activity is detailed for three different investments—one money market fund, one company stock fund, and one index fund. The stock fund referred to is a mini-mutual fund that contains only one holding—company stock, a common method used among companies that allow their employees to invest in company stock. In addition to company stock, the mini-fund typically holds a small cash component, which provides greater liquidity for trades and more flexibility than if individual company shares were sold directly to plan participants. The employee's balance in the mini-fund is a function of the number of units held times the unit share price; the unit share price, of course, rises and falls directly based on the company's stock price, which is provided for information purposes.

The last column totals the figures for all of the funds in the plan in which the participant is invested.

The opening balance at the top of the account activity section and the closing balance at the bottom provides the market value of the employee's investments at the opening and closing day of the statement period. In between these two balances, the statement describes how the participant went from the opening balance to the closing balance:

- Contributions: Dollar amounts contributed to each of the funds, usually listed by the source—either the employee or the employer. Some statements may

Figure 1. 401(k) Plan Statement Example

PAT PARTICIPANT
123 MAIN STREET
LOUISVILLE KY 40220-1253

STATEMENT PERIOD:
4/01/XX to 6/30/XX

ACCOUNT VALUE
AS OF 06/30/XX
$7,793.17

ACTIVITY THIS PERIOD

	Money Market Fund	Company Stock Fund	Index Fund	TOTAL
OPENING BALANCE	$523.00	2,863.24	$4,250.46	$7,636.70
SHARES/UNITS	523.000	280.435	101.540	
SHARE/UNIT PRICE	$1.00	$10.21	$41.86	
CONTRIBUTIONS				
EMPLOYEE PRE-TAX BASIC			$238.01	$238.01
EMPLOYER			$238.01	$238.01
TOTAL CONTRIBUTIONS			$476.02	$476.02
LOAN PAYMENTS	$0.00	$0.00	$0.00	$0.00
LOAN INTEREST	$0.00	$0.00	$0.00	$0.00
TRANSFERS/ROLLOVERS IN	$0.00	$0.00	$0.00	$0.00
TRANSFERS/ROLLOVERS OUT	$0.00	$0.00	$0.00	$0.00
LOAN WITHDRAWALS	$0.00	$0.00	$0.00	$0.00
FEE WITHDRAWALS	$0.00	$0.00	$0.00	$0.00
DIVIDENDS AND CAP. GAINS	$19.87	$19.37	$22.34	$61.58
MARKET GAIN/LOSS	$0.00	$375.79-	$5.34-	$381.13-
CLOSING BALANCE	$542.87	$2,506.82	$4,743.48	$7,793.17
SHARES/UNITS	542.870	284.866	113.453	
SHARE/UNIT PRICE	$1.00	$8.80	$41.81	
COMPANY STOCK PRICE		$34.63		
APPROXIMATE STOCK SHARES		72.40		
NET OF LOAN(S)				$7,793.17
VESTED VALUE				$7,325.58

CURRENT CONTRIBUTIONS ALLOCATION

	EMPLOYEE PRE-TAX BASIC	EMPLOYER
INDEX FUND	100.0%	100.0%

SUMMARY OF CONTRIBUTIONS

SOURCE	YEAR TO DATE	CURRENT VALUE
EMPLOYEE PRE-TAX BASIC	$476.02	$2,856.12
EMPLOYER	$476.02	$2,856.12
EMPLOYEE ROLLOVER	$.00	$2,080.93
TOTAL	$952.04	$7,793.17

Source: Based on a statement provided by The Vanguard Group

break down these contributions even further, for instance, employer-matched contributions.
- Loan activity (if any): Some companies allow participants to borrow limited amounts from their plan. If this has occurred, such transactions may be detailed here. This can include an employee's repayments for outstanding loans, interest payments to the plan by the employee on the outstanding loan (this interest rate is determined by the employer), and/or loan withdrawals.
- Transactions: Transactions that occurred during the statement period are detailed on separate lines. These include: fund exchanges—transferring assets from one investment to another within the plan; transfers/rollovers—assets that are either rolled over or transferred into the plan from a different trustee or a different plan; and withdrawals (assets that are withdrawn from the account).
- Dividends and Cap. Gains: Dividends, interest income, and capital gains paid to and reinvested in the account.
- Market Gain/Loss: The change in the market value of the investments during the period covered by the statement.

The closing balance in the last column is the total value of the participant's 401(k) plan—the "account value" noted at the top of the statement. However, this value is not necessarily the current bottom line real value to the participant.

Vested Value: The Real Bottom Line

Two other factors affect the real value of the plan to the participant:
- Outstanding loans (if any): If a participant has borrowed from the plan, those monies must be repaid. The closing balance on the statement most likely will include the monies owed to the plan; a *net of loans* figure states the closing balance less all outstanding loans to the participant and represents dollars that are actually currently invested in the various funds of the plan.
- Vesting: Many 401(k) plans have vesting requirements for monies contributed by the employer. Vesting is the right an employee gradually acquires to receive employer-contributed benefits, and it is based on the length of time he is employed by the company. The amount by which you are vested in a plan represents the percentage of employer-contributed assets to which you would be entitled if you were to leave the company at that point in time. For instance, if you are 100% vested and you leave your company, you have the right to all (100%) of the value of the assets represented by contributions made by the employer into the 401(k) plan; if you are 90% vested and you were to leave the company, you would receive 90% of the value of the assets represented by those contributions. Of course, if you remain with the company, you would eventu-

ally become fully vested.

You are always 100% vested in any money that you, the employee, contribute to the plan. The last line in this section of Figure 1 notes the *vested value* of this participant's plan. This amount is lower than the closing balance value, which means that this participant is not yet fully vested. If she were to leave the company at the end of this statement period, the amount she would be entitled to is $7,325.58. The vested value is the true value of the plan to the participant at this point in time. While many plans have vesting requirements on employer contributions, some have immediate full vesting. If this is the case, a *vested value* line may not appear on the statement. If in doubt, check with your plan administrator.

Other Statement Information

The sample statement contains two other sections:
- The current contributions allocation states how you are currently allocating employee and employer contributions among the plan's investment options.
- The summary of contributions provides the current value of the contributions that have been made by the employee and the employer. Aside from simply providing information on the source of contributions, this section also indicates how much you are vested in the plan. In the example in Figure 1, the employer's contributions to the plan currently are valued at $2,856.12, while $4,937.05 represents the employee's contributions [$2,856.12 + $2,080.93]. Of the vested value of the plan, $2,388.53 represents the employer's portion [$7,325.58 − $4,937.05]. That means that this employee is about 84% vested in the plan [$2,388.53 ÷ $2,856.12]. However, you can also call the plan administrator to find out the percentage in which you are vested in the plan—probably an easier route.

What Is Your Return?

Many participants want to know the rates of return they are receiving on their investments. This may or may not be provided on the statement. If you are invested in mutual funds, simply look up the return for each fund among the many sources that track mutual fund performance. For investment options in which information does not appear in widely published sources, use the equation in the box on the next page, which provides a return approximation.

The equation assumes that withdrawals and contributions are relatively evenly distributed over the investment period; if you have made a large contribution or withdrawal relative to the total value of the fund during the time period covered, the approximation equation will be less accurate.

The example at the bottom of the equation determines the return for the index fund in Figure 1 for the time period covered by the statement, which is the second quarter of the year. The return approximation could also be used to determine the return for the entire plan.

Calculating Your Return: An Approximation

$$\left[\frac{\text{End Balance} - 0.50(\text{Net Additions})}{\text{Beginning Balance} + 0.50(\text{Net Additions})} - 1.00 \right] \times 100 = \text{Return (\%)}$$

End Balance: Balance at end of statement period. Note that this automatically includes any interest or dividends reinvested (not withdrawn). You do **not** need to add these to the end balance.

Beginning Value: Balance at beginning of statement period.

Net Additions: Contributions, transfers, and rollovers into the account less all withdrawals, transfers, and rollovers out of the account. If withdrawals are greater than additions, this number will be negative.

Example using the Index Fund in Figure 1:

$$R\% = \left[\frac{\$4{,}743.48 - 0.50(\$476.02)}{\$4{,}250.46 + 0.50(\$476.02)} - 1.00 \right] \times 100$$

$$= \left[\frac{\$4{,}505.47}{\$4{,}488.47} - 1.00 \right] \times 100$$

$$= [1.0038 - 1.00] \times 100$$

$$= 0.38\% \text{ for period covering 2nd quarter}$$

Understanding 401(k) Mechanics: A Look at How the Plans Operate

Given the importance of a 401(k) investment to one's retirement nest egg, it is necessary to understand the mechanics of a 401(k) plan to confirm that your contributions are properly deposited into your 401(k) on a timely basis and in the investment choices you have selected, and that your plan is being administered properly.

This chapter will look at 401(k) plans from the standpoint of the information that is available to you and what should be made available to you from your employer, what to do if you do not receive the appropriate information, and how to make sure your contributions are properly deposited.

Background

Traditional defined-benefit retirement plans were structured to provide a monthly retirement sum to an employee if the person met the necessary requirements in terms of years of service to have a vested benefit. Most employees paid little or nothing into these plans; employers bore all of the costs and were mandated to fund the plans by a federal law, ERISA, passed in 1974. However, employers have in recent years shifted their focus to 401(k) plans to save money and to encourage their employees to save. In effect, the burden of amassing enough retirement assets has shifted from employers to employees.

Chapter 4 explained how 401(k) plans operate. To briefly recap:

An employee participant first designates how much he wishes to contribute on a pretax basis. This has the advantage of reducing the employee's salary for income tax (but not for Social Security tax) purposes. The employee usually has available some investment vehicles to which he may allocate his contributions. The employer may even match some of the contribution, which may be allocated to company stock if the company so wishes, or to one of the investment choices selected by the employee. The dollars deposited into the plan grow on a tax-deferred basis until retirement.

Employees have the ability to take their vested accumulated plan assets with them when they leave their employer; these assets can remain in a tax-deferred account either by depositing them into the new employer's plan or into an IRA, or the employee can take distribution of the assets by paying taxes and a 10% penalty for early withdrawal if they are under age 59½.

Employers like 401(k) plans because of reduced fiduciary liability and plan costs. Investment of the assets becomes the employee's "problem" and not that of the employer.

Who Runs the Plan?

401(k) plans generally involve a structure consisting of the company, a recordkeeper, a trustee/custodian, investment vehicles managed by an outside money manager, and, possibly, an investment consulting firm. The representatives of the company usually consist of the human resources department and a management-selected committee responsible for overseeing the plan. The human resources area advertises the plan to the employees, deducts the contributions from paychecks and transmits the money to the trustee. The committee is charged with ensuring the proper administration of the plan in an oversight mode.

Corporate use of outside administrators ("outsourcing") has proved popular recently because it shifts the burden of doing all or most of the work to an outside vendor. Costs may even be lower with outsourcing. However, outsourcing does not end the responsibility of the company to monitor the plan and ensure that it is being properly administered by the outside vendor(s).

Recordkeepers are hired to keep track of the cash inflows, outflows, and employee loans from the plan. They also keep the plan participants' accounting records for their investment in the plan and are responsible for sending the participants periodic reports of their 401(k) assets, or forwarding the reports to the employer for mailing to the participants. Recordkeepers also carry out the non-discrimination testing that is legally required of plans on a periodic basis. This testing is done to determine the participation rate of lower-paid employees in the plan. Since a 401(k)'s pretax deduction feature is particularly favorable to higher-paid employees and executives, the government wants more lower-paid workers in the plan so that the plan is not a "perk" or tax avoidance for the more highly paid. Failure to pass the test results in a reduced contribution rate for the more highly paid employees, possibly resulting in some of the deducted dollars being handed back to them, thus increasing their taxable income.

Some small companies do their own recordkeeping. We shall see later that this can raise a warning flag to employees in companies that might be tempted to use the employees' contributions in the business.

A trustee/custodian is hired to make disbursements from the plan, take contributions from the employees and to hold the plan's assets. The trustee/custodian is also used to pay bills to outside vendors for services rendered to the plan. This firm is generally a bank or a trust company.

Outside money managers are hired to provide the investment options made available

> **Information That Must Be Given to 401(k) Plan Participants**
>
> - *Employee enrollment form*: To be filled out by the employee, this indicates the percentage amount the employee wants to contribute to the plan and how the employee wants contributions allocated among the investment options.
>
> - *Summary Plan Description*: Abbreviated listing of plan provisions, including vesting rules for employer contributions, distribution rules, and grievance procedures.
>
> - *Information on investment options (upon enrollment in plan, and in periodic reports)*: Regulatory definitions are sketchy, and the amount of information varies from company to company. Firms using mutual funds usually provide prospectuses and periodic reports.
>
> - *Periodic Financial Statements*: Reflecting the participant's account, including contributions, any outstanding loans, income earned, capital gains and losses, plus the beginning and ending balance.

to the participants. These providers consist of mutual fund families, bank commingled trusts, and investment advisory boutique firms offering individually-managed accounts. Of these, the trend is definitely for some form of commingled fund managed by banks, insurance companies and/or mutual fund families.

Some plan sponsors employ the services of different vendors, adopting a "mix and match" approach of, say, one recordkeeper, a different trustee and mutual funds from various fund families. This allows the plan to choose from the best available in each category. However, a more recent trend has been for 401(k) plans to use a "bundled" approach. This basically means one-stop shopping—a company can go to the XYZ family of funds and find all of the plan's needed services available under one roof. This has the advantage of simpler administration and no need to expend time selecting various vendors. A disadvantage is that one fund family might not have the best mutual funds in each asset class. In that case, ease of administration could come at the expense of outstanding performing funds not available in that particular asset class of the bundled fund family. Another variation on a bundled product is an "alliance" in which a recordkeeper will offer multiple mutual fund families to a plan sponsor along with other needed services. This has the advantage of allowing a company to select mutual funds from a wide variety of choices, perhaps even a broad spectrum of outstanding funds. A disadvantage is the somewhat higher cost to the plan.

The last player in the 401(k) may be an investment consulting firm that provides services similar to those provided to defined-benefit plans—performance measurement and monitoring, portfolio manager and investment style review, and recommended changes to the investment options offered to the plan participants to replace a poorly performing fund or to expand options for participants. However, consultants are not used as much on 401(k) plans as they are on defined-benefit plans.

All of the above players incur a fiduciary responsibility when providing services to a 401(k) plan and can possibly be sued if the services are negligently carried out or there is incompetence or fraud. An employer may reduce (but not eliminate) his fiduciary responsibility by adopting the Department of Labor's 404(c) regulations and offering at least three different investment options with distinctively different risk and return characteristics, which when combined would create a diversified portfolio with reduced risk. In addition, the employer must allow the participants to transfer assets among the options at least once every 90 days. While adopting the 404(c) safe harbor regulations reduces the employer's fiduciary responsibility, that action does not eliminate all responsibility. Employers are still responsible for proper administration and management of the plan and for using due diligence in hiring outside service providers.

What Documents Should Plan Participants Receive?

No employee can be forced to participate in a 401(k), but those who choose to do so must be given:
- Employee enrollment forms,
- A Summary Plan Description (SPD), and information on the investment options.

On the employee enrollment form, the employee indicates the percentage of his paycheck that he wishes deducted under the tax-free limit and the investment options to which he wants to allocate his ongoing contributions. Some plans allow aftertax contributions to the plan; these dollars grow on a tax-deferred basis but are included as a separate category on the employee's periodic statements.

The Summary Plan Description is an abbreviated listing of the plan provisions (the plan's "mechanics") and describes various items such as the vesting rules for any employer matching of contributions, distribution rules, and grievance procedures. In addition, the Summary Plan Description offers the complete plan document for a fee—a valuable offer if an employee wants to appeal an employer decision or contest some part of the 401(k) plan.

While employers must provide information on the plan's investment choices, the regulatory definition of appropriate material is sketchy at best. Employers are loathe to do anything that might smack of investment advice, a situation that would increase their fiduciary liability if an employee sues. Firms that use mutual funds usually provide fund prospectuses and the fund's semiannual reports.

Investment education is another problem; companies do not want to be investment advisers to their employees. One solution has been to hire vendors who create videos or use humorous situations to try to make investment managers out of ordinary, non-financial people. Another answer is the creation by mutual fund families of so-called "Lifestyle" funds. Three or four balanced strategies are crafted to cater to different investors. Thus, a young person would supposedly choose an aggressive balanced approach while an older person would supposedly select a more conservative balanced approach.

What About Ongoing Information?

Of course, 401(k) plan participation is an ongoing process, and therefore employers must provide participants with two types of reports:
- Periodic financial statements reflecting the person's particular account, and
- Periodic reports on the investment options.

The periodic financial reports include: beginning balances, contributions, loan amounts, income earned, capital gains and losses, and ending balances. You should carefully review these reports to verify their accuracy. You may not know the income or gains/losses numbers, but you do know your contribution amounts from your paychecks. Keep in mind that even with the most honest employer there will probably be a delay after the end of the recording period of up to six weeks. Delays do not equal malfeasance.

The periodic reports on your plan balances may or may not break out the amounts you contributed and your employer matched, and there is no legal requirement for an employer to separate the two balances. If your employer makes a matching contribution in company stock, that balance will show up as a separate line on the periodic report. If the employer makes a match using the same investment options you have chosen, it will be harder to differentiate the balances if they are not broken out in the report. You should keep track of your contributions so that you will have some idea of the approximate amount that is yours. In addition, be sure you know the vesting policy if you receive an employer match. Plan participants immediately vest in their own contributions and in the earnings on their contributions. However, you may or may not immediately vest in any matching contributions made by your employer; the employer may legitimately delay full vesting for a number of years (up to seven). If you plan to leave the company, have a substantial amount residing in the employer's matching contribution, and are very close to vesting, you might want to stay at that employer to vest in the employer's match.

Investment option information must also be reported to participants. This can take the form of official reports from mutual fund families or digested material from the employer or recordkeeper. In many cases, employees receive only perfunctory performance information sometimes with an offer to receive an updated or annual report, if so desired and requested. If your employer makes such an offer, take him up on it and read the additional material carefully.

Receipt of these reports should trigger a review of your overall asset allocation and cause you to consider any changes to your asset mix and/or your contributions. You always have the option to make switches among the options and to change the allocation of your contributions. Use the reports to cause a re-evaluation.

What Problems Can Occur?

Certain problems can occur with a 401(k) plan. These include:
- Errors in plan administration,
- Failure to effect transfers expeditiously, and
- Fraud or negligence, but it is important to keep in mind that this is extremely rare.

Errors can occur with any recordkeeper. There is no way you can independently check on the reputation of an outside recordkeeper. But if you detect an error, contact your human resources department with full details on your claim. Retroactive corrections will occur providing that you can demonstrate that an error occurred. Pay stubs are a good place to start.

Problems with transfers can be more problematical. Most plans employ daily valuation so that a participant can find out each day what her account is worth and in many cases can effect transfers each day through an 800 number prior to the close of business (4 p.m. Eastern time for mutual funds). Some plans only allow transfers at the end of a month or a quarter. This has the advantage of lower costs for the plan and reduced opportunities for participants to try to time the market on a short-term basis (probably a good thing). However, as a participant you should be aware of when telephoned transfer instructions are actually effected. An egregious example occurred before the October 1987 stock market crash. On September 30, a number of investors instructed their plans to transfer their stock positions to less volatile investment options; however, the plan administrators, in keeping with the plan's provisions, effected the transfers at the end of October, after the market drop! It pays to know the transfer rules. Fraud and negligence are extremely rare—the overwhelming majority of plans (almost 100%) are administered with the employee's good in mind. But what if you suspect that yours is not?

The first thing to look for is the existence of an outside recordkeeper. If there is one, you should be more confident in the plan and your employer. If your statements come from your employer and are perennially late or have numerous errors, you can question the human resources department as to their recordkeeping procedures and ask for an accounting verification (audit trail) of the plan. A legitimately run plan will not hesitate to accede to your requests.

Employees should remember that employers have up to 90 days to deposit the participants' contributions into the plan. So you should keep in mind that failure to make an immediate deposit is clearly within federal law and regulations and is not necessarily a sign of fraud.

Should you suspect a violation of the law and/or the plan, you can complain to the Pension and Welfare Benefits representative located in your local Department of Labor office. Be sure that you have sufficient facts to justify your accusation. Threatening to sue on your own by claiming violation by the employer or one of the vendors of their fiduciary responsibility just won't work. You are better off going to the government.

What if You are Dissatisfied With the 401(k) Plan?

Let's say that you are unhappy with the investment choices offered in the plan or want the plan liberalized to allow more frequent transfers. What can you do?

The only logical option is to present your human resources department with a cogent reason for changing managers, adding new funds, or making changes in the plan. The odds that you will succeed are slim unless you convince a large percentage of your fellow workers to support you. Keep in mind that the more liberal the plan, the higher the costs, and these costs are ultimately borne by the participants.

Plan costs are a difficult issue to grapple with because of the myriad of fees (e.g., management, recordkeeping, trustee, and consulting) and the fact that companies do not have to divulge the plan's fees. The one fee you can learn about is the management fee ("expense ratio") for a mutual fund by reading the prospectus. More and more companies are starting to pass on all of the plan's fees to the participants. You might be able to detect the fee level if the fees are detailed on your periodic financial reports. Protesting fees, however, will generally get you nowhere.

Conclusion

If you are eligible for and participate in a 401(k) plan, you should scrutinize the plan with the same care as you would for any investment.

But you should also make sure that you understand the mechanics of the plan, so that you can make the best use of it, and to ensure that the plan is being administered properly. Great investment vehicles cannot outweigh a plan design that does not work in your interest.

The ABCs of GICs in Retirement Investing

Guaranteed investment contracts, or GICs, are one of the most popular choices of participants in 401(k) retirement plans, who collectively hold $200 billion of these securities. Approximately two-thirds of all 401(k) plans offer GICs as an investment option, and GICs account for more than 50% of the invested assets of these plans.

Despite their popularity, these investment alternatives are not well understood by many investors. Yet a thorough knowledge of GICs, including their risks and potential returns, is important for anyone seriously considering them.

GIC Basics

GICs are similar to certificates of deposit, except that they are marketed by insurance companies. With GICs, the investor pays money in exchange for a contract that "promises" the return of principal at maturity plus an investment yield that is in line with prevailing money market rates at the inception of the contract. The yields on GICs are generally higher than those on CDs by one-half of a percent to one percentage point at the time of purchase.

Insurance companies, in turn, invest GIC money in a variety of instruments—mortgages; government, corporate and high-yield bonds; and private placements.

There are two basic types of GICs—participating and non-participating. With the first variety, investors receive a variable rate of return, and thus they participate in the risks and rewards resulting from interest rate fluctuations. Non-participating GICs offer a fixed rate of return.

When current interest rates are high, it may make sense to buy a non-participating GIC and lock in the high fixed rate of return for the life of the contract. However, if interest rates are expected to rise, it may instead be preferable to invest in a participating GIC.

GICs and 401(k) Plans

GICs are not marketed to individual investors, but rather to corporate investors. Corporate investors, in turn, use them as an investment alternative for their retirement plan assets. Thus, although individuals don't purchase GICs directly, they are frequently offered the option of investing in GICs through their corporate retirement plans, in particular, the increasingly common 401(k) plans.

In a 401(k) plan, it is the employee who makes the investment decision among the options offered by the company. A company that sponsors a 401(k) plan must offer at least three options for investing their pension contributions; typical options are a money market fund, the company's stock, one or more equity funds, and a GIC.

For the portion of 401(k) plan assets allocated by employees to GICs, the company's pension plan manager shops among the insurance companies that offer GICs, looking for attractive interest rates and maturities.

GIC contracts purchased for defined-contribution pension plans, including 401(k)s, are generally quite large. A standard transaction might involve $10 million or more. The contracts generally have a maturity of between one and seven years. When the term of the GIC contract is up, the employees' pension fund recovers the principal and either reinvests it in another GIC or returns it to employees who are retiring or cashing out of the plan.

To diversify the risk of GICs, fund managers may sign contracts with as many as 20 issuers, although one recent study suggested that the typical large employer purchased GICs from seven different carriers. The yield that an employee receives on his or her investment represents the blended rate of return from the various GICs.

Principal Risks—No Guarantee

One reason for the popularity of GICs is the assumption by investors that the risk of loss of principal is eliminated. After all, aren't these investments "guaranteed"? The answer is no. The "guarantee" refers only to the rate of interest that the issuer promises to pay for the life of the contract. The principal is very much at risk if the issuer fails.

In contrast to CDs issued by banks that are federally insured (for up to $100,000), GICs are backed by the financial health of the insurance company issuing the contract, not by the federal government. Therefore, a GIC is only as good as the insurance company that issues it. Recently, some insurance companies, burdened with junk-bond investments and non-performing real estate loans, have seen their creditworthiness deteriorate. The well-publicized failures of Executive Life and Mutual Benefit Life in 1991 have forced pension fund managers and 401(k) plan members to take a harder look at GICs.

Of course, the chance that big insurance companies will go bankrupt and cost employees their 401(k) money is not very large. This risk is further reduced if the company's plan is invested in GICs issued by a number of insurance companies, since the failure of one insurer would not necessarily cause a significant drop in the value of the pension plan's assets. Moreover, many major insurance companies that market GICs hold only small amounts of non-investment grade, or junk, bonds. About 50% of the junk bonds owned by the life insurance industry are held by 10 companies, and few of these companies sell GICs. Thus, the assets backing the GICs are invested in relatively safe investments.

On the other hand, certain questions remain. In particular, where in line does an investor's principal stand if the insurance company that issued a GIC goes bankrupt? Currently, the laws in most states provide that holders of GICs come after policyholders should an insurer go bankrupt. Other than Louisiana, all states maintain a guarantee fund to repay policyholders in the event of insurance company failures. Not all state funds, however, cover GICs. Half the states are not specific on this question.

Newer Varieties

The traditional GIC issued by insurers promises a return based on the earnings of the company's assets, but the principal is backed by the company's ability to pay—in short, its own creditworthiness. The popularity of GICs combined with concerns over the financial soundness of insurance companies have prompted the development of new versions of guaranteed investment contracts by other types of institutions.

The new varieties of GICs carry extra protection against default by issuers. These include so-called BICs, or bank investment contracts, which are sold by such institutions as Bankers Trust and J.P. Morgan, and GIC "alternatives" which are issued by major securities firms such as Merrill Lynch, Putnam, and Shearson Lehman Brothers.

Unlike owners of guaranteed investment contracts issued by insurance companies, investors in contracts marketed by banks and investment firms purchase the underlying securities outright. The securities are then held in trust for investors. That clearly puts the securities beyond reach of the banks' and investment firms' creditors in case of default, thereby spreading the risk beyond the contract's issuer. Some banks deposit additional securities as collateral to make up any shortfall in the market value of the original investments in case of default, whereas some investment firms guarantee the book value of the contract by obtaining an irrevocable letter of credit.

Investors might assume that BICs would be protected by FDIC insurance. In principle, bank investment contracts are bank deposits and therefore can be federally insured for as much as $100,000. However, it's up to the banks to decide whether FDIC insurance is offered, and few banks offer FDIC insurance on BICs. The cost of the premiums, about ¼%, would make the product less competitive with non-FDIC insured GICs if passed along to buyers, and less profitable to the financial institutions if not. Thus, some investors are continuing to stick with traditional GICs issued by the most creditworthy issuers because of the higher returns.

BICs face stiff competition from a variety of other GIC alternatives. The securities firms, along with some insurers, are promoting an alternative instrument known as a synthetic GIC. With synthetics, an employer is permitted to see what's in the portfolio of investments and, in some instances, can choose the specific assets that back the contract. Thus, rather than relying on all of an issuer's portfolio, the investor, for example, could pick mortgages backed by Fannie Mae or Treasuries, which are virtually risk-free as far as principal repayment. Under this arrangement, should the issuer become insolvent, the assets designated for the guaranteed investment contracts are transferred back to the pension fund.

Although synthetic GICs shift the credit risk away from the issuer, buyers pay for the sense of added security. Gone from synthetic GICs is the long-term guaranteed rate of return. Instead, these securities have annual interest rate adjustments. Moreover, buyers assume at least some of the default risk of the underlying investments. If an investment in a synthetic GIC soured, the investor's yield would be reduced.

Individual Investors and GICs

As described in Chapter 6, an employee who participates in a company's 401(k) plan is legally entitled to annual reports from his plan manager on how his investments are performing.

What should you look for if a GIC is an option? First, examine the names of the insurance companies that sold the GICs. If this information is not contained in the annual plan report or some other plan description, ask a representative of the pension plan. Most companies, sensitive to employees' concerns, will supply credit-rating information on the GICs they hold.

If your firm won't provide credit-rating information, you can get it yourself from several sources. Chief among the insurance company rating services is A.M. Best, which puts out a number of publications covering the insurance industry. "Best's Insurance Reports" (Life/Health) lists ratings for about 1,500 insurance companies on a scale of A+ to C–. The report also tells the percentage of non-investment grade bonds that a GIC issuer holds. Other ratings can be found in Moody's Insurance Credit Report and Standard & Poor's Insurer Solvency Review; these reports along with Best's Insurance Reports are available in most public libraries.

Pension plans should buy GICs from companies rated A+ (Superior), and A or A– (Excellent) by A.M. Best. If you find a carrier rated less than A– by Best on your company's list, you should request an explanation of why the company is undertaking such a risk.

In addition to the level of credit rating, you should also examine the list for diversification among a number of insurance companies. The company should be buying GICs from at least three separate insurance companies.

Are GICs Appropriate?

Some experts question whether GICs yield enough to be suitable investments for retirement plans. In general, the yields on GICs/BICs are slightly higher than those prevailing on Treasury securities of comparable maturities. As with other fixed-rate investments, the yields increase as the term to maturity increases. Yields also go up as the size of the GIC contract increases.

How should you analyze GICs when making an allocation decision? GICs are very similar to bonds, and share a similar shortcoming—they may not provide a long-term return that can keep pace with inflation. This subjects the investor to the risk that he may outlive his retirement benefits. By concentrating on the credit and market risk associated with GICs, investors may be overlooking this very serious risk.

Even if a GIC is performing well, an investor under age 40 can probably afford to accept greater levels of market risk. The rationale for younger investors to undertake greater market risk is explained by the potential for greater reward offered by alternative investment mediums over long time periods. For example, a diversified portfolio of common stocks has generated a compounded annual return of roughly 15% over the last 15 years. For an initial $10,000 investment, the difference over a 15-year investment horizon between this return and the 8% return from a non-participating GIC is $49,650. Investors who are under 40 should therefore consider placing between 70% and 80% of their retirement portfolio into common stocks.

On the other hand, returns on common stocks are also considerably more volatile year-by-year than GICs. As a result, for individuals closer to retirement who may need access to some cash for living expenses within a few years, a gradual shift of a portion of pension monies into fixed-income securities (such as GICs, CDs, or short-term Treasuries) may be useful, although it is important even in retirement to keep a portion of assets (around 50%) in growth investments such as equities.

Such a retirement strategy has the benefit of growth fueled by the stock market when the investor can afford to take greater risk during younger days, tempered somewhat by the safety of fixed-income instruments at the time of retirement when taking chances with the stock market becomes a somewhat risky venture.

IRAs: One Other Retirement Choice

Individual retirement accounts have always been popular, and recent tax law changes dramatically expanded the application and opportunity for increasing tax-favored individual savings through the use of IRAs. What are the choices? Here's a brief rundown.

Individual Retirement Accounts

Individual retirement accounts (IRAs) provide an opportunity for some taxpayers to defer compensation. IRA contributions up to $2,000 ($4,000 in the case of a spousal IRA when one spouse has little or no income from employment) may be fully deducted by a working taxpayer as long as:
- Neither the taxpayer nor the taxpayer's spouse is covered by an employer-sponsored retirement plan, or
- The tax taxpayer or the taxpayer's spouse is covered by an employer-sponsored plan, but joint adjusted gross income does not exceed a certain amount.

Beginning in 1998, the income levels for the phaseout will increase (see Table 3). If these conditions are satisfied, the contribution is deductible even if you do not itemize deductions, thus causing the tax result to be similar to that of a 401(k) plan contribution. As with a 401(k) plan, the money and earnings in a deductible IRA and a traditional non-deductible IRA are not taxed until you withdraw them.

Withdrawals before age $59^1/_2$ are generally subject to a 10% early withdrawal penalty, in addition to the regular income tax payable on the distribution. There are exceptions, however, to the 10% additional tax (but not income tax) on early withdrawals from IRAs for withdrawals used to pay qualified higher-education expenses and for qualified first-time home buyers. Qualified higher-education expenses include tuition, fees, books, supplies, room and board, and equipment expenses. A qualified first-time homebuyer distribution is a withdrawal of up to $10,000 during the individual's lifetime that is used within 120 days to pay costs (including reasonable settlement, financing, or other closing costs) of acquiring, constructing, or reconstructing the principal residence of a first-time homebuyer. This exception is available for the first-time homebuyer expenses of the individual, spouse, child, grandchild, or ancestor of such individual or spouse.

Spousal IRAs

Separate IRA accounts can be established for each spouse. The total $4,000 spousal IRA contribution can be allocated between the spouses in any proportion as long as the amount allocated to one spouse does not exceed $2,000. However, the combined contribution cannot be higher than the combined earnings of the spouses in the year the contribution is made.

Non-deductible IRAs, Roth IRAs

Even if you do not satisfy the requirements that allow a tax deduction for your IRA contribution, you may still contribute up to $2,000 (less any deductible IRA contributions) to a traditional non-deductible IRA. (The contribution may be up to $4,000 for a spousal IRA.) Although the contribution is not deducted from taxable income, the earnings on the contribution are not taxed until they are withdrawn. This often-overlooked opportunity can provide significant benefits if used consistently for several years.

There is also a new category of non-deductible IRA called the Roth IRA. The Roth IRA is funded solely with aftertax (non-deductible) contributions, but unlike current non-deductible IRAs, it exists as a separate account and offers the possibility of tax-free earnings.

The principal features of the Roth IRA are as follows:
- No tax deduction is allowed for contributions to the account.
- Income accumulates tax-free in the account.
- Qualified distributions from the account are not included in income.
- Income limitations for contributions begin at $150,000 for married taxpayers filing jointly and $95,000 for single taxpayers.
- The maximum contribution is coordinated with the deductible IRA and is limited annually to the maximum IRA contribution allowed for that individual.
- Contributions can be made even if the individual is beyond age 70½.
- No distributions are required when the individual attains age 70½.
- Distributions are only required upon death.
- Rollovers are permitted from one Roth IRA to another Roth IRA.

Non-taxable qualified distributions from a Roth IRA include distributions made at least five years after the first taxable year in which the individual made a contribution to the Roth IRA, if they are made: (1) after the individual reaches age 59½; (2) after death; (3) on account of disability; or (4) for qualified first-home purchases. Non-qualified distributions are includible in income to the extent of earnings after recovery of contributions, and are subject to the additional 10% early withdrawal tax.

The Education IRA

An Education IRA is a separate IRA account for the benefit of a named beneficiary that has the intended purpose of providing funds for the attendance in a program of higher education. Like the Roth IRA, this account is created without providing an income tax deduction for the contribution. However, the earnings of this account are subject to inclusion in gross income and the additional 10% tax upon distribution to the extent the distribution exceeds qualified higher-education expenses.

The Education IRA has the following principal features:
- Contributions of up to $500 annually are allowed (which is in addition to the $2,000 regular IRA limit).
- Contributions may be made regardless of whether the beneficiary has gross income.
- Contributions may not be made after the beneficiary attains age 18.
- Distributions of income from the account are included in income and subject to the additional 10% tax to the extent they exceed qualified higher education expenses.
- Income limitations for contributions begin at $150,000 for married taxpayers filing jointly and $95,000 for single taxpayers.

It would appear from the language used in the law that up to 19 contributions could be made for a child if you begin contributions at birth. The last contribution would have to be made in the calendar year the beneficiary turns 18, but on or before the beneficiary's birthdate. The following example demonstrates a likely balance of an Education IRA at age 18, assuming a maximum annual contribution of $500 is made each year on the beneficiary's birthday and the account provides an 8% annual rate of return:

Age	Value	Contributions
Birth	$ 500	$ 500
5	$ 3,668	$ 3,000
10	$ 8,323	$ 5,500
15	$ 15,162	$ 8,000
18	$ 20,723	$ 9,500

In the above example, the entire investment balance of $20,723, plus on-going earnings, could be used to pay qualified higher education expenses. To the extent the funds distributed exceed those expenses, the *earnings* on the account would be includible ratably in income and are subject to the additional 10% tax. The amount may be transferred to the Education IRA of another family member or another qualifying family member can be designated as beneficiary. Although the Education IRA is

Table 1.
Comparing IRAs:
Same Tax Rate in Year of Contribution and Withdrawal
(32% in year of contribution and withdrawal)

Assumptions: Cash contributions for the IRA, Roth IRA, non-deductible IRA, and corporate bond represent the contributions available subsequent to taxes being assessed at some previous time. The rate of return on the investments is 8% compounded annually. The ending withdrawals from the IRAs are not subject to the additional 10% penalty tax. The year-one tax savings amounts shown for the deductible IRA grow at an 8% rate of return compounded annually. The growth of the year-one tax savings are subject to a tax rate equivalent to the year of contribution until the final year when the withdrawal rate applies. Tax rates were calculated as combined federal and state tax rates using federal rates of 28% and 15% and state rates of 5% and 4%, respectively. The state rates are applied to the federal rates on an aftertax basis for total combined tax rates of 32% and 18%.

	Cash Contribution ($)	Gross Funds After 10 Years ($)	Net Funds Avail in Year 10 on First-Year Tax Savings ($)	Taxes Due in Year 10 ($)	Net Funds Available After Tax in Year 10 ($)	Winners
Deductible IRA	2,000	4,318	1,087	1,382	4,023	
Roth IRA	2,000	4,318	—	—	4,318	✔
Non-deductible IRA	2,000	4,318	—	742	3,576	
Corporate Bond	2,000	3,397	—	—	3,397	

technically a non-deductible tax-deferred IRA, it is in essence a functional equivalent of the Roth IRA to the extent of qualified higher-education expenses.

Choosing Your Options

Suppose a taxpayer has saved $2,000 of aftertax funds in 1998 and is looking to move those funds into one of the IRA investments. How does that person decide which of these tax-advantaged plans to use, or whether to invest in a taxable instrument such as a corporate bond? Which option is the "winner" in terms of aftertax return on investment? In answering these questions, it is important to consider the limitations still in place for investment in an IRA and determine that this is an available option. Assuming that a taxpayer is not limited, the following example demonstrates some of the differences and similarities of the possible investment options.

As Tables 1 and 2 demonstrate, all three IRA options would earn $2,318 after 10 years, leaving the taxpayer with $4,318 of gross funds. The corporate bond would earn about $900 less over that same period because of the annual taxation of interest income. The deductible IRA, Roth IRA, and non-deductible IRA all leave the taxpayer with more in net aftertax funds in year 10 than the corporate bond, but that is not the

Table 2.
Comparing IRAs:
Lower Tax Rate in Year of Withdrawal
(32% in year of contribution, 18% in year of withdrawal)

Assumptions: Cash contributions for the IRA, Roth IRA, non-deductible IRA, and corporate bond represent the contributions available subsequent to taxes being assessed at some previous time. The rate of return on the investments is 8% compounded annually. The ending withdrawals from the IRAs are not subject to the additional 10% penalty tax. The year-one tax savings amounts shown for the deductible IRA grow at an 8% rate of return compounded annually. The growth of the year-one tax savings are subject to a tax rate equivalent to the year of contribution until the final year when the withdrawal rate applies. Tax rates were calculated as combined federal and state tax rates using federal rates of 28% and 15% and state rates of 5% and 4%, respectively. The state rates are applied to the federal rates on an aftertax basis for total combined tax rates of 32% and 18%.

	Cash Contribution ($)	Gross Funds After 10 Years ($)	Net Funds Avail in Year 10 on First-Year Tax Savings ($)	Taxes Due in Year 10 ($)	Net Funds Available After Tax in Year 10 ($)	Winners
Deductible IRA	2,000	4,318	1,099	777	4,640	✔
Roth IRA	2,000	4,318	—	—	4,318	
Non-deductible IRA	2,000	4,318	—	417	3,901	
Corporate Bond	2,000	3,433	—	—	3,433	

whole story. The deductible IRA is a more valuable investment than the non-deductible IRA because the $2,000 aftertax investment in the deductible IRA provides a first-year tax benefit of $640 ($2,000 multiplied by the 32% tax rate). This money represents a tax savings in year one that may be invested in a taxable investment with compounding growth opportunity until the end of year 10 (the year of withdrawal in the example). Thus, the taxpayer using the deductible IRA benefits to the extent of the compounded aftertax earnings of the $640 invested for 10 years in addition to the inside tax-deferred growth of the IRA. In contrast, the non-deductible IRAs (including the Roth IRA) receive no current-year tax savings. Despite the aftertax growth of the first-year tax savings, the Roth IRA is the clear winner, assuming equal tax rates in the year of contribution and distribution, because no tax is due on withdrawal with this account.

On the other hand, if the tax rate in the year of withdrawal is lower than in the year of contribution, then the deductible IRA is the clear winner with the Roth IRA as the runner-up. This scenario represents a typical retirement planning expectation that tax rates will be lower in the year of withdrawal.

The three types of IRAs outperform the aftertax investment in the corporate bond in both Tables 1 and 2. However, other factors unrelated to taxes may make some non-tax-favored investments more attractive (that is, the flexibility to withdraw funds without incurring penalties, the ability to invest more than the IRA annual contribution limit, etc.). Therefore, when choosing an investment, many factors unique to the individual taxpayer must be considered. Those factors include, but are not limited to, applicable tax rates at contribution, expected tax rates at distribution, available rates of investment return, and desired flexibility of the investment.

Summary

Individuals have many options to fund retirement, a child's education, and a first home purchase. Before you take advantage of these benefits, though, make sure that you understand the ramifications of your choices given your individual situation, and have a clear picture of how each vehicle fits into your personal financial plan.

Deductible IRAs will continue to have tremendous appeal to taxpayers, particularly when future tax rates during retirement may be lower than tax rates in those years contributions are being made.

Table 3 provides a summary of the rules relating to deductibility of IRA contributions.

Table 3.
A Guide to Deducting IRA Contributions

1999 limitation amounts are reflected in the table, with annual adjustments through 2007 in the section below.

	Scenario One	Scenario Two	Scenario Three
Contributor Participates in employer-sponsored qualified retirement plan	No	No	Yes
Spouse Participates in employer-sponsored qualified retirement plan	No	Yes	Yes or No
IRA is Deductible ...	Yes	Sometimes (see below)	Sometimes (see below)
IRA is Deductible if Adjusted Gross Income (AGI) Is Below These Amounts for:			
—Married Filing Joint Taxpayers		$150,000	$50,000
—Single Taxpayers		N/A	$30,000
IRA Deduction is Phased Out for AGI Between These Amounts for:			
—Married Filing Joint Taxpayers		$150,000–$160,000	$50,000–$60,000
—Single Taxpayers		N/A	$30,000–$40,000
IRA is Non-Deductible for AGI Over this Amount for:			
—Married Filing Joint Taxpayers		$160,000	$60,000
—Single Taxpayers		N/A	$40,000

The phaseout ranges in Scenario Three will continue to grow as follows:

	Single Taxpayers	Married Filing Joint Taxpayers
1999	$31,000–$41,000	$51,000–$61,000
2000	$32,000–$42,000	$52,000–$62,000
2001	$33,000–$43,000	$53,000–$63,000
2002	$34,000–$44,000	$54,000–$64,000
2003	$40,000–$50,000	$60,000–$70,000
2004	$45,000–$55,000	$65,000–$75,000
2005	$50,000–$60,000	$70,000–$80,000
2006	$50,000–$60,000	$75,000–$85,000
2007 and thereafter	$50,000–$60,000	$80,000–$90,000

Planning Considerations With the Roth IRA

The Roth IRA provides another powerful weapon in the taxpayer's arsenal of tax-favored retirement planning vehicles. There are two ways to make contributions to a Roth IRA: through non-deductible cash contributions, or by converting assets in a traditional IRA. A traditional IRA is either a deductible or non-deductible IRA as defined before the 1997 Tax Act.

Because the relatively low income limitations preclude many people from being eligible to make *deductible* contributions to a traditional IRA, the decision of whether to make annual contributions to a Roth IRA is greatly simplified. The more difficult decision (and far more important for many taxpayers), is whether an existing traditional IRA should be converted to a Roth IRA. This decision involves considerations related to tax, retirement, estate, and investment allocation planning and may be influenced by numerous interrelated factors. This is the central focus of this chapter.

Annual Contributions

Beginning in 1998, up to $2,000 annually can be contributed to a Roth IRA if modified adjusted gross income (AGI) is:
- No more than $95,000 for single taxpayers.
- No more than $150,000 for joint returns (a spouse may also contribute up to $2,000 annually as long as the couple's combined earned income is at least equal to the contributed amount).
- If you are married but filing a separate tax return you may contribute a portion of the $2,000 maximum contribution amount if your adjusted gross income does not exceed $15,000. However, a proposed technical correction provision may reduce this amount to $10,000.

Although contributions are not deductible, withdrawals from the account are non-taxable if they are made after you reach age 59½, and if at least five years have elapsed since the first Roth IRA contribution was made.

Unlike contributions to a traditional IRA, contributions to a Roth IRA can be made even if you are a participant in a qualified plan such as a 401(k), and even after you reach age 70½.

Limitations On Converting

Beginning in 1998, you may convert existing traditional IRAs into a Roth IRA during any tax year in which your adjusted gross income does not exceed $100,000. The same $100,000 limit applies whether you are single or married filing a joint return (married individuals filing separate returns are not eligible to convert regardless of their income level). "Adjusted gross income" for purposes of conversion does not include any taxable income recognized as a result of a conversion to a Roth IRA. In addition, beginning in year 2005, minimum required distributions from any type of plan are also excluded. Your adjusted growth income is on line 32, at the bottom of your Form 1040.

Although the AGI limitation may initially eliminate you from converting, you may be able to "manage" your income and expenses to keep your adjusted growth income at or below the $100,000 threshold.

For example, a retired taxpayer with significant investment income might shift a large portion of his or her investments to either tax-free municipal bonds or one-year Treasury bills payable after December 31 of the year of conversion. Closely-held business owners might consider shifting income into tax years immediately before or after the year of conversion or pulling deductions into the year of conversion from tax years immediately before and after the year of conversion. Both employees and business owners might reduce their adjusted gross income by increasing their contributions to qualified retirement plans during the year of conversion. Of course, managing income and expenses shouldn't be done to the extent that you have insufficient assets or income to fund living expenses during the conversion year.

If you convert a traditional IRA to a Roth IRA and your income exceeds the $100,000 AGI limitation, you may essentially reverse the transfer any time up to the extended due date of the tax return for the year of conversion. The specific wording of the statute actually allows transfers from one type of IRA to any other type of IRA for any reason, not exclusively in the situation where adjusted growth income exceeds the $100,000 limitation. This creates an opportunity to lock-in a conversion value at or near the lowest IRA account value during the year of conversion. For example, if you convert (or have already converted) your traditional IRA at a time when the IRA account value is high, and your IRA account value subsequently declines in value, you may transfer the converted Roth IRA back to a traditional IRA, and then reconvert to a Roth IRA at the lower IRA account value.

A direct conversion from a qualified retirement plan, such as a 401(k) plan or a defined-benefit plan, is not allowed. If you have such plans, you would need to first rollover the qualified plan into a traditional IRA and then convert to a Roth IRA. Unfortunately, this is not possible if you are currently employed by the company sponsoring the plan. However, if you have a 401(k) plan with a previous employer, it typically can be converted to a traditional IRA at any time.

Should You Convert?

There are several major factors that will have an impact on any decision to convert. These include:

Your Tax Bracket in the Years of Conversion and in Year of Distribution

The conversion from a traditional IRA to a Roth IRA will cause the amount converted to be included in your gross income for the year(s) of conversion to the extent that it would otherwise be taxable if taken as a traditional IRA distribution. Your marginal income tax rate in both the year(s) of conversion and the years of future distributions is a critical factor in assessing whether a traditional IRA should be converted to a Roth IRA.

It is interesting to note that there is no difference between paying the income taxes at the "front end" (i.e., making a conversion) or paying the taxes at the "back end" (i.e., not converting) if the marginal income tax rate when making contributions is the same as the tax rate when distributions are taken.

For example, if a fully taxable traditional IRA with a $2 million balance is converted to a Roth IRA, and the applicable marginal income tax rate is 39.6%, income taxes of $792,000 will reduce the balance in the Roth IRA to $1,208,000. After ten years of growth at an 8% rate of return, the $1,208,000 will grow to $2,607,981. On the other hand, if the traditional IRA is not converted, the account will grow (over the same period of time and at the same rate of return) to $4,317,850. Once the taxes of $1,709,869 are paid (again, based on a 39.6% rate), the remaining balance is $2,607,981, the same as the converted Roth IRA. [This example intentionally ignores other benefits of the Roth IRA that would in fact result in a disparity between traditional and converted Roth IRAs, such as the ability to pay the income taxes resulting from the conversion with funds outside the IRA, or the additional deferral benefits of not being required to take minimum distributions prior to the participant's death. These factors are discussed later.]

However, if the marginal income tax rate at the time of conversion differs from the rate at the time of distribution, a disparity in the overall benefits will occur.

If you are in a higher tax bracket in the year(s) of conversion than you expect to be in the years of distribution (likely if you convert during your working years), the net aftertax benefits favor the traditional IRA.

For example, a fully taxable $2 million traditional IRA converted at a 39.6% marginal tax rate would result in an income tax liability of $792,000 leaving $1,208,000 in the Roth IRA. At an 8% compound annual rate of return over 10 years, the Roth IRA will grow to $2,607,981, all of which can be withdrawn completely income tax-free. If the $2 million traditional IRA is not converted, the IRA will grow to $4,317,850, assuming the same 8% compound annual rate of return over 10 years. If the applicable marginal tax rate declines to 31% at the time of withdrawal, a tax liability of $1,338,534 would be owed resulting in a net balance of $2,979,317.

Therefore, keeping the traditional IRA (i.e., not converting) results in $371,336 of additional aftertax funds. The larger the tax rate differential, the larger the benefit of keeping the traditional IRA.

A decline in tax rates could occur from either a decrease in income in later years or a change in state residence by the taxpayer. Consider, for example, a taxpayer currently working in California or New York who is subject to a marginal state income tax rate of 8% to 10%. If he or she retires to Texas, Florida, or Nevada (which have no state income taxes), the taxpayer's overall tax rate is more likely to be lower, perhaps significantly lower. This common scenario would significantly reduce the benefits of converting to a Roth IRA.

On the other hand, if a taxpayer is in a lower tax bracket in the contemplated year(s) of conversion than he or she expects to be in the years of distribution, the net aftertax benefits favor the Roth IRA.

For example, a $2 million traditional IRA converted at a 36% marginal tax rate would result in an income tax liability of $720,000, leaving $1,280,000. At an 8% compound annual rate of return over 10 years, the Roth IRA will grow to $2,763,424, all of which can be withdrawn completely income tax-free. If the $2 million traditional IRA is not converted, the IRA will grow to $4,317,850, assuming the same 8% compound annual rate of return over 10 years. If the applicable marginal tax rate increases to 39.6% by the time of withdrawal, a tax liability of $1,709,869 would be owed, resulting in a net balance of $2,607,981. In this example, converting to a Roth IRA results in $155,443 of additional aftertax funds. The larger the tax rate differential, the larger the benefit of converting to a Roth IRA.

The result of conversion may be additional taxable income, which can push you into a higher income tax bracket. This tax result may be lessened if the conversion occurred in 1998 due to a special rule that allows the tax liability resulting from a 1998 conversion to be spread ratably over four years. You would report 25% of the conversion income on your tax returns for years 1998–2001. The four-year spread applies automatically unless the taxpayer specifically elects not to have it apply.

The impact of additional taxable income resulting from a conversion may impact the availability of other tax benefits, such as the new child or education credits, or the new deduction for interest expense on a loan for higher education expenses. It would also increase the itemized deduction phaseout that is based on adjusted gross income. The loss of these credits and deductions for a conversion year(s) must be weighed against the long-term tax benefits of a Roth IRA.

Finally, one last consideration is the likelihood that tax rates will simply change. Unfortunately, this is a factor that taxpayers have no control over, and which cannot be easily predicted. In the case of taxpayers who do not plan to take distributions from their IRA for many years, the conversion to a Roth IRA could have detrimental consequences if the federal tax structure was significantly altered, for example, to a flat tax or a national sales tax system.

Source of Payment of Conversion Tax Liability

The source of funds for paying the conversion tax can also have a significant impact on your decision of whether or not to convert to a Roth IRA.

If you can pay the income tax liability arising from a conversion with assets *outside* of your IRA, you may benefit greatly. Paying the tax with non-IRA dollars is equivalent to making an additional contribution to the IRA in the amount of the tax paid. As a result, you have increased the total amount of investments receiving the IRA "tax benefit."

As illustrated earlier, there is no difference between paying the income taxes at the "front end" (i.e., making a conversion) or paying the taxes at the "back end" (i.e., not converting) if the taxes are paid from the IRA proceeds. Recall that in both situations a taxpayer in the 39.6% tax bracket with a $2,000,000 IRA earning 8%, would have $2,607,981 after 10 years. However, if the taxpayer is able to pay the conversion tax liability with funds outside the IRA, the Roth IRA will grow to $4,317,850 after 10 years. Compare this amount to a traditional IRA with a $792,000 "side account" (to represent the conversion taxes paid from non-IRA sources); the traditional IRA grows to $2,607,981, and the "side account" grows (at a 5% aftertax rate of return) to $1,290,085, for a total of $3,898,066 after 10 years. Therefore, by paying the "conversion tax" with funds from outside the IRA, the taxpayer accumulates an additional $419,784 after taxes.

Of course, if you have other deductible qualified retirement plans to which you could otherwise make contributions, up to the amount equal to the tax liability arising from the conversion, the benefits of conversion would be reduced (i.e., in the case where you can only fund one or the other, not both). In addition, to the extent you could contribute to a 401(k) program and receive an employer-matching contribution, the decision not to convert (and instead contribute to the 401(k) plan) may yield greater overall benefits. In other words, paying the tax with non-IRA dollars is like making *additional* IRA contributions.

Conversion will be more beneficial to taxpayers who can pay the conversion taxes with assets outside their traditional IRA, and who do not have access to deductible qualified retirement plans to which they can make additional contributions. High wage earners who have "maxed out" their qualified retirement plans, and retired taxpayers (without access to qualified retirement plans) may be the most likely candidates.

Minimum Distribution Requirements Prior to Death

Perhaps the most powerful benefit of converting to a Roth IRA is the additional tax-deferral benefits over and above those of a traditional IRA. A Roth IRA, unlike a traditional IRA, does not require minimum distributions until after your death (traditional IRAs require minimum annual distributions once you reach age 70½). If you are married at the time of death, the Roth IRA may be rolled over by your surviving spouse into his or her own Roth IRA, without any required distributions until your surviving spouse's death.

The benefits of additional tax deferral during your life (and your surviving spouse's life) can be astounding, especially for taxpayers who do not need to take withdrawals for living expenses, and who wish to maximize the amount of wealth passing to heirs. Both of these situations are fairly common.

For example, consider two taxpayers, John and Bob, each age 55. They are both married and each have $2 million in traditional IRAs. Each desires to pass their entire IRA to their heirs because they have sufficient other resources for their retirement living expenses. Assume John decides not to convert to a Roth IRA, but Bob converts to a Roth IRA and pays the taxes with funds outside of his IRA. Assume further that all IRA assets earn an 8% compound annual rate of return, and that both taxpayers are currently in, and will remain in, the 39.6% federal income tax bracket.

As a result of the required minimum distribution rules, John must begin to take distributions each year beginning at age 70½, and pay the corresponding income tax on each distribution. If John lives to age 90, and required minimum distributions are calculated using joint life expectancy (assuming John's spouse is the same age as John) with no annual recalculation of their life expectancy, his IRA account will be completely distributed by age 90 (of course, John would have accumulated the "aftertax annual distributions" over the years). To make an accurate comparison to Bob, a "side fund" for John would exist with an initial balance equal to Bob's conversion tax liability of $792,000 ($2 million × 39.6%). Assuming an aftertax return of 5% on both the aftertax accumulated distributions fund and the side fund, John will have a total of $19,225,566 at age 90 ($14,856,882 from the accumulated distributions fund, and $4,368,684 from the side fund).

Because Bob is not required to take any distributions, his account grows to $31,936,344 by age 90. Thus, Bob will have an additional $12,710,778 of taxable estate for his heirs by converting to a Roth IRA!

The benefits of additional tax deferral, however, do not necessarily stop at your death. The minimum distribution rules that take effect upon the death of a participant are the same for both traditional and Roth IRAs, and may allow continued deferral by allowing an IRA account to be distributed over the life expectancy of your "designated" beneficiary(ies).

Other Withdrawal Considerations

Any amount distributed from a Roth IRA is characterized in the following order

based upon the value of the account as of the end of the taxable year:
- First, from *annual* contributions to the Roth IRA (to the extent that all previous distributions from the Roth IRA have not yet exceeded the contributions);
- Second, from *"converted"* contributions on a first-in, first-out basis; if a particular converted contribution is being analyzed, the dollars that were includible in gross income by virtue of the conversion come out before non-taxable dollars come out; and
- Third, from earnings.

A taxpayer may generally withdraw contributions to a Roth IRA at any time without tax or penalty. Contributions, in this context, include any amount that was converted from a traditional IRA. There are, however, two exceptions to this rule:
- First, if income caused by a 1998 conversion is spread over a four-year period and a distribution is made anytime during the first three years, such distribution results in an acceleration of the recognition of the deferred income to the extent that it would have been taxed in a later year as a result of the four-year spread.
- Second, with respect to amounts converted (regardless of whether or not the conversion income is spread over four years), if a distribution is made before a five-year period beginning January 1 of the calendar year in which the conversion is made, such distribution is subject to a 10% penalty tax (unless an exception applies) to the extent that the distributed amount would have been taxable if it had been distributed from the traditional IRA and not converted to a Roth IRA. [The 10% penalty tax does not apply if: the taxpayer is 59½ or older; dies; becomes disabled; uses the distributed funds to purchase his or her first home (up to $10,000); receives substantially equal periodic payments; uses the distributed funds to pay medical expenses above 7½% of his or her AGI; uses the distributed funds to pay insurance premiums while unemployed; or uses the distributed funds to pay higher education expenses.]

Earnings in a Roth IRA may be distributed income tax-free if they are withdrawn on or after age 59½, and after a five-year period beginning on January 1 of the tax year in which the first contribution (whether "annual" or "converted") is made to the Roth IRA. Any distribution of earnings made prior to age 59½, but after the five-year holding period, and that occurs as a result of the taxpayer's death or disability, or that is used to purchase a first home (up to $10,000), is also income tax-free. In addition, any distributions of earnings made prior to age 59½ is subject to a 10% penalty tax (unless one of the exceptions noted above applies) regardless of whether the five-year holding period has been satisfied.

Estate Tax Considerations

For wealthy taxpayers subject to estate taxes, the conversion of a traditional IRA to a Roth IRA will reduce their taxable estate by the amount of income taxes paid as a result of such conversion. For example, consider a taxpayer subject to a 35% marginal income tax rate (federal and state) and a 55% estate tax rate with a $2 million traditional IRA and an estate of $5 million. If the taxpayer converts the traditional IRA before his or her death, income tax of $700,000 will be due, thereby reducing the taxpayer's taxable estate by $700,000, and saving $385,000 in estate taxes.

If the same taxpayer dies without converting the $2 million traditional IRA, the entire account constitutes "income in respect of a decedent," does not receive a step-up in tax basis, and therefore, is subject to both estate and income taxes. The recipient of the traditional IRA is allowed a miscellaneous itemized income tax deduction (not subject to the 2% of adjusted gross income floor) for any estate taxes paid on the IRA, however, the deduction is only for federal (not state) estate taxes, and is subject to the 3% phaseout of itemized deductions.

Conversion of a traditional IRA will also be beneficial if that IRA is being used to fund a credit shelter trust to ensure both spouses' applicable estate tax exemption amounts are fully utilized. Funding a credit shelter trust with a Roth IRA allows the ultimate recipients to receive such assets free from both estate and income taxes.

Social Security Considerations

Considerations surrounding Social Security benefits might also impact your decision of whether or not to convert a traditional IRA to a Roth IRA. A conversion may subject a larger portion of your Social Security benefits to taxation as a result of the taxable income that must be recognized in any year in which a conversion is made (or over four years if the conversion was made in 1998).

However, you may still benefit overall (even if a greater portion of Social Security benefits is subject to taxation in the year(s) of conversion) since Roth IRA withdrawals are not subject to tax if they satisfy the special earnings withdrawal rule. For example, once you convert a traditional IRA, and pay the resulting income tax, all future distributions from the Roth IRA are excluded from taxable income. Additionally, none of the funds are subject to the minimum distribution rules imposed on traditional IRAs at age 70½; this may allow you to reduce (or perhaps avoid) income tax on your Social Security benefits.

The Downside: Uncertainty

Because the Roth IRA is new, the rules governing its treatment (both tax and non-tax) are uncertain and subject to change. Congress has addressed numerous initial uncertainties through technical corrections and recently issued regulations. However, because the Roth IRA is so new, there are likely to be some factors and aspects that simply will not be fully known and understood for some time.

Consider that in many states, Roth IRAs do not currently enjoy the same protection from creditors afforded traditional IRAs. The reason is that most state statutes specifically refer to Internal Revenue Code section 408, and Roth IRAs are allowed under a new code section, 408A. It is expected that most state legislatures will act quickly to provide Roth IRAs with the same creditor protection as traditional IRAs, but until such time, this could be a concern for certain taxpayers.

Taxpayers should also verify that their state conforms to federal law with respect to the tax treatment of Roth IRAs. Otherwise, IRA funds could be subject to state taxation at the time of conversion from a traditional IRA, and when funds are ultimately withdrawn from the Roth IRA.

Another concern that many people have expressed is the possibility that Congress could simply change its mind about the taxation of Roth IRAs. One author, Richard J. Werts, in "The Promise of No New Taxes—Will We Ever Learn?" has expressed this concern in noting:

". . . we only need to look to the history of the Social Security Act and Administration to see an uncanny example of an about-face by the Congress on the tax-free promises of deferred withdrawals. The Social Security tax itself is a "forced" Roth-like retirement deferral . . . the contributions are aftertax (i.e., no net taxable benefits occur due to "contributions") and the "withdrawals," in the form of Social Security benefits upon disability or retirement, were tax-free. Tax-free, that is, until the clever and reasonable argument was made that people with other incomes SHOULD pay tax on their Social Security benefits. After all, they are getting much more out than they put in. Exactly the position that all of us will be in when we wish to begin liquidating our Roth IRAs."

In addition to simply subjecting Roth IRAs to taxation, Congress could make other changes that would impact the overall benefits of Roth IRAs by, for example, applying the same minimum distributions rules applicable to traditional IRAs once a participant reaches age 70½, accelerating the recognition of Roth IRA funds at the death of the participant—(thereby removing the benefit of additional tax-free deferral over the lives of designated beneficiaries), or characterizing Roth IRA distributions as "alternative minimum tax" preference items.

There is, of course, always the possibility that Roth IRAs already in existence would be grandfathered from any future tax law changes, but unfortunately, it is never certain whether such grandfather provisions will provide sufficient protection of all current benefits.

Maximizing The Benefits

Once you have determined that you qualify to convert your traditional IRA, and that you should in fact do so, the next question (of potentially considerable importance) is *when* should you convert? You should carefully consider the timing (and amount) of your conversion(s) so as to maximize the benefits of conversion.

If you intend to retire in a few years and will be in a lower tax bracket at that time, delaying conversion of your IRA could be beneficial.

Conversion over two or more years might be advised in an effort to reduce the impact of the graduated tax structure by converting just enough assets so as not to trigger the imposition of a higher tax bracket.

If you intend to use at least some portion of your traditional IRA assets to pay for living expenses during your retirement, but also desire to pass some portion to heirs, the optimal plan might call for conversion of only a portion of the traditional IRA. Your objective is to avoid mandatory withdrawals in excess of income needs due to the minimum distribution rules applicable to traditional IRAs. The optimal plan in this situation would involve two stages. During the first stage of retirement, income is provided exclusively from the traditional IRA in compliance with the minimum distribution rules. The goal during this stage is to completely consume the traditional IRA before the last to die of you and your spouse.

During the second stage, the Roth IRA is used to fund retirement income needs after the traditional IRA has been depleted. The optimal plan will thereby free you from the escalating minimum distribution requirements and allow all remaining account assets to pass to heirs completely income tax-free.

Therefore, by determining your income needs over these two stages, you might maximize your overall benefits by converting only the amount of the current traditional IRA needed to satisfy living expenses during the first stage of retirement.

Conclusion

Because so many factors may influence the decision of whether to convert a traditional IRA to a Roth IRA, you need to give careful consideration to the overall impact of numerous and competing factors. There is simply no substitute for crunching the numbers, under multiple scenarios. Even then, the conversion decision depends, to some extent, on your ability to accurately "predict" your personal and financial status in the future, as well as the future tax and legal environment.

To briefly summarize, the following factors will generally tip the scales:

Factors in Favor of Converting
- You intend to transfer the bulk of your IRA to heirs; avoidance of the required

minimum distribution rules at age 70½ results in greater accumulation of IRA assets that may pass to heirs.
- You are able to pay the conversion tax liability from sources outside your IRA account.
- You anticipate being subject to a higher marginal income tax rate during the years you make distributions from the IRA account.

Factors in Favor of Not Converting
- You anticipate being subject to a lower marginal income tax rate during the years you take distributions from the IRA account.
- You have significant fears or expectations that Congress will change the laws in such a way that Roth IRAs will be negatively impacted.

Because the conversion decision can impact tax, retirement, estate, and investment allocation planning, you may want to consult your financial planning professional.